Practical Grammar Composition

Thomas Wood

Alpha Editions

This edition published in 2024

ISBN 9789361470721

Design and Setting By

Alpha Editions
www.alphaedis.com

Email - info@alphaedis.com

As per information held with us this book is in Public Domain.
This book is a reproduction of an important historical work.
Alpha Editions uses the best technology to reproduce historical work
in the same manner it was first published to preserve its original nature.
Any marks or number seen are left intentionally to preserve.

Contents

PREFACE	- 1 -
CHAPTER I	- 3 -
CHAPTER II	- 8 -
CHAPTER III	- 14 -
CHAPTER IV	- 34 -
CHAPTER V	- 49 -
CHAPTER VI	- 106 -
QUESTIONS FOR THE REVIEW OF GRAMMAR	- 113 -
A GENERAL EXERCISE ON GRAMMAR	- 115 -
CHAPTER VII	- 121 -
CHAPTER VIII	- 140 -
CHAPTER IX	- 150 -
CHAPTER X	- 156 -
CHAPTER XI	- 176 -
CHAPTER XII	- 186 -
GLOSSARY OF MISCELLANEOUS ERRORS	- 227 -

PREFACE

This book was begun as a result of the author's experience in teaching some classes in English in the night preparatory department of the Carnegie Technical Schools of Pittsburg. The pupils in those classes were all adults, and needed only such a course as would enable them to express themselves in clear and correct English. English Grammar, with them, was not to be preliminary to the grammar of another language, and composition was not to be studied beyond the everyday needs of the practical man.

Great difficulty was experienced because of inability to secure a text that was suited to the needs of the class. A book was needed that would be simple, direct and dignified; that would cover grammar, and the essential principles of sentence structure, choice of words, and general composition; that would deal particularly with the sources of frequent error, and would omit the non-essential points; and, finally that would contain an abundance of exercises and practical work.

It is with these ends in view that this book has been prepared. The parts devoted to grammar have followed a plan varying widely from that of most grammars, and an effort has been made to secure a more sensible and effective treatment. The parts devoted to composition contain brief expositions of only the essential principles of ordinary composition. Especial stress has been laid upon letter-writing, since this is believed to be one of the most practical fields for actual composition work. Because such a style seemed best suited to the general scheme and purpose of the book, the method of treatment has at times been intentionally rather formal.

Abundant and varied exercises have been incorporated at frequent intervals throughout the text. So far as was practicable the exercises have been kept constructive in their nature, and upon critical points have been made very extensive.

The author claims little credit except for the plan of the book and for the labor that he has expended in developing the details of that plan and in devising the various exercises. In the statement of principles and in the working out of details great originality would have been as undesirable as it was impossible. Therefore, for these details the author has drawn from the great common stores of learning upon the subjects discussed. No doubt many traces of the books that he has used in study and in teaching may be found in this volume. He has, at times, consciously adapted matter from other texts; but, for the most part, such slight borrowings as may be discovered have been made wholly unconsciously. Among the books to which he is aware of heavy literary obligations are the following excellent texts: Lockwood and Emerson's Composition and Rhetoric, Sherwin Cody's Errors in Composition, A. H. Espenshade's Composition and Rhetoric, Edwin C. Woolley's Handbook of Composition, McLean, Blaisdell and Morrow's Steps in English, Huber Gray Buehler's Practical Exercises in English, and Carl C. Marshall's Business English.

To Messrs. Ginn and Company, publishers of Lockwood and Emerson's Composition and Rhetoric, and to the Goodyear-Marshall Publishing Company, publishers of Marshall's Business English, the author is indebted for their kind permission to make a rather free adaptation of certain parts of their texts.

Not a little gratitude does the author owe to those of his friends who have encouraged and aided him in the preparation of his manuscript, and to the careful criticisms and suggestions made by those persons who examined the completed manuscript in behalf of his publishers. Above all, a great debt of gratitude is owed to Mr. Grant Norris, Superintendent of Schools, Braddock, Pennsylvania, for the encouragement and painstaking aid he has given both in preparation of the manuscript and in reading the proof of the book.

T.W.

BRADDOCK, PENNSYLVANIA.

CHAPTER I

SENTENCES.—PARTS OF SPEECH.—ELEMENTS OF THE SENTENCE.—PHRASES AND CLAUSES

1. In thinking we arrange and associate ideas and objects together. Words are the symbols of ideas or objects. A **Sentence** is a group of words that expresses a single complete thought.

2. Sentences are of four kinds:

1. **Declarative;** a sentence that tells or declares something; as, *That book is mine.*

2. **Imperative;** a sentence that expresses a command; as, *Bring me that book.*

3. **Interrogative;** a sentence that asks a question; as, *Is that book mine?*

4. **Exclamatory;** a declarative, imperative, or interrogative sentence that expresses violent emotion, such as terror, surprise, or anger; as, *You shall take that book!* or, *Can that book be mine?*

3. Parts of Speech. Words have different uses in sentences. According to their uses, words are divided into classes called Parts of Speech. The parts of speech are as follows:

1. **Noun;** a word used as the name of something; as, *man, box, Pittsburgh, Harry, silence, justice.*

2. **Pronoun;** a word used instead of a noun; as, *I, he, it, that.*

Nouns, pronouns, or groups of words that are used as nouns or pronouns, are called by the general term, **Substantives**.

3. **Adjective;** a word used to limit or qualify the meaning of a noun or a pronoun; as, *good, five, tall, many.*

The words *a, an,* and *the* are words used to modify nouns or pronouns. They are adjectives, but are usually called **Articles**.

4. **Verb;** a word used to state something about some person or thing; as, *do, see, think, make.*

5. **Adverb;** a word used to modify the meaning of a verb, an adjective, or another adverb; as, *very, slowly, clearly, often.*

6. **Preposition;** a word used to join a substantive, as a modifier, to some other preceding word, and to show the relation of the substantive to that word; as, *by, in, between, beyond.*

7. **Conjunction;** a word used to connect words, phrases, clauses, and sentences; as, *and, but, if, although, or.*

8. **Interjection;** a word used to express surprise or emotion; as, *Oh! Alas! Hurrah! Bah!*

Sometimes a word adds nothing to the meaning of the sentence, but helps to fill out its form or sound, and serves as a device to alter its natural order. Such a word is called an **Expletive.** In the following sentence *there* is an expletive: ***There*** *are no such books in print.*

4. A sentence is made up of distinct parts or elements. The essential or **Principal Elements** are the Subject and the Predicate.

The **Subject** of a sentence is the part which mentions that about which something is said. The **Predicate** is the part which states that which is said about the subject. *Man walks.* In this sentence, *man* is the subject, and *walks* is the predicate.

The subject may be simple or modified; that is, may consist of the subject alone, or of the subject with its modifiers. The same is true of the predicate. Thus, in the sentence, *Man walks,* there is a simple subject and a simple predicate. In the sentence, *The good man walks very rapidly,* there is a modified subject and a modified predicate.

There may be, also, more than one subject connected with the same predicate; as, ***The man and the woman*** *walk.* This is called a **Compound Subject**. A **Compound Predicate** consists of more than one predicate used with the same subject; as, *The man* ***both walks and runs.***

5. Besides the principal elements in a sentence, there are **Subordinate Elements.** These are the Attribute Complement, the Object Complement, the Adjective Modifier, and the Adverbial Modifier.

Some verbs, to complete their sense, need to be followed by some other word or group of words. These words which "complement," or complete the meanings of verbs are called **Complements**.

The **Attribute Complement** completes the meaning of the verb by stating some class, condition, or attribute of the subject; as, *My friend is a* **student**, *I am* **well**, *The man is* **good** *Student, well,* and *good* complete the meanings of their respective verbs, by stating some class, condition, or attribute of the subjects of the verbs.

The attribute complement usually follows the verb *be* or its forms, *is, are, was, will be,* etc. The attribute complement is usually a noun, pronoun, or adjective, although it may be a phrase or clause fulfilling the function of any of these parts of speech. It must not be confused with an adverb or an adverbial modifier. In the sentence, *He is **there**, there* is an adverb, not an attribute complement.

The verb used with an attribute complement, because such verb *joins* the subject to its attribute, is called the **Copula** ("to couple") or **Copulative Verb**.

Some verbs require an object to complete their meaning. This object is called the **Object Complement**. In the sentence, *I carry a **book***, the object, *book*, is required to complete the meaning of the transitive verb *carry*; so, also in the sentences, *I hold the **horse**,* and *I touch a **desk**,* the objects *horse* and *desk* are necessary to complete the meanings of their respective verbs. These verbs that require objects to complete their meaning are called Transitive Verbs.

Adjective and **Adverbial Modifiers** may consist simply of adjectives and adverbs, or of phrases and clauses used as adjectives or adverbs.

6. A **Phrase** is a group of words that is used as a single part of speech and that does not contain a subject and a predicate.

A **Prepositional Phrase**, always used as either an adjective or an adverbial modifier, consists of a preposition with its object and the modifiers of the object; as, *He lives **in Pittsburg**, Mr. Smith **of this place** is the manager **of the mill**, The letter is **in the nearest desk**.*

There are also Verb-phrases. A **Verb-phrase** is a phrase that serves as a verb; as, *I **am coming**, He **shall be told**, He **ought to have been told**.*

7. A **Clause** is a group of words containing a subject and a predicate; as, *The man **that I saw** was tall.* The clause, *that I saw*, contains both a subject, *I*, and a predicate, *saw*. This clause, since it merely states something of minor importance in the sentence, is called the **Subordinate Clause**. The **Principal Clause**, the one making the most important assertion, is, *The man was tall*. Clauses may be used as adjectives, as adverbs, and as nouns. A clause used as a noun is called a **Substantive Clause**. Examine the following examples:

> Adjective Clause: The book *that I want* is a history.
> Adverbial Clause: He came *when he had finished with the work*.
> Noun Clause as subject: *That I am here* is true.
> Noun Clause as object: He said *that I was mistaken*.

8. Sentences, as to their composition, are classified as follows:

Simple; a sentence consisting of a single statement; as, *The man walks.*

Complex; a sentence consisting of one principal clause and one or more subordinate clauses; as, *The man that I saw is tall.*

Compound; a sentence consisting of two or more clauses of equal importance connected by conjunctions expressed or understood; as, *The man is tall and walks rapidly*, and *Watch the little things; they are important.*

EXERCISE 1

In this and in all following exercises, be able to give the reason for everything you do and for every conclusion you reach. Only intelligent and reasoning work is worth while.

In the following list of sentences:

(1) Determine the part of speech of every word.

(2) Determine the unmodified subject and the unmodified predicate; and the modified subject and the modified predicate.

(3) Pick out every attribute complement and every object complement.

(4) Pick out every phrase and determine whether it is a prepositional phrase or a verb-phrase. If it is a prepositional phrase, determine whether it is used as an adjective or as an adverb.

(5) Determine the principal and the subordinate clauses. If they are subordinate clauses, determine whether they are used as nouns, adjectives, or adverbs.

(6) Classify every sentence as simple, complex, or compound.

1. Houses are built of wood, brick, stone, and other materials, and are constructed in various styles.
2. The path of glory leads but to the grave.
3. We gladly accepted the offer which he made.
4. I am nearly ready, and shall soon join you.
5. There are few men who do not try to be honest.
6. Men may come, and men may go, but I go on forever.
7. He works hard, and rests little.
8. She is still no better, but we hope that there will be a change.
9. Let each speak for himself.
10. It was I who told him to go.
11. To live an honest life should be the aim of every one.

12. Who it really was no one knew, but all believed it to have been him.

13. In city and in country people think very differently.

14. To be or not to be, that is the question.

15. In truth, I think that I saw a brother of his in that place.

16. By a great effort he managed to make headway against the current.

17. Beyond this, I have nothing to say.

18. That we are never too old to learn is a true saying.

19. Full often wished he that the wind might rage.

20. Lucky is he who has been educated to bear his fate.

21. It is I whom you see.

22. The study of history is a study that demands a well-trained memory.

23. Beyond the city limits the trains run more rapidly than they do here.

24. Alas! I can travel no more.

25. A lamp that smokes is a torture to one who wants to study.

EXERCISE 2

(1) *Write a list of six examples of every part of speech.*

(2) *Write eight sentences, each containing an attribute complement. Use adjectives, nouns, and pronouns.*

(3) *Write eight sentences, each containing an object complement.*

(4) *Write five sentences, in each using some form of the verb* **to be**, *followed by an adverbial modifier.*

CHAPTER II

NOUNS

9. A noun has been defined as a word used as the name of something. It may be the name of a person, a place, a thing, or of some abstract quality, such as, *justice* or *truth*.

10. Common and Proper Nouns. A **Proper Noun** is a noun that names some particular or special place, person, people, or thing. A proper noun should always begin with a capital letter; as, *English, Rome, Jews, John*. A **Common Noun** is a general or class name.

11. Inflection Defined. The variation in the forms of the different parts of speech to show grammatical relation, is called **Inflection**. Though there is some inflection in English, grammatical relation is usually shown by position rather than by inflection.

The noun is inflected to show number, case, and gender.

12. Number is that quality of a word which shows whether it refers to one or to more than one. **Singular Number** refers to one. **Plural Number** refers to more than one.

13. Plurals of singular nouns are formed according to the following rules:

1. Most nouns add *s* to the singular; as, *boy, boys; stove, stoves*.

2. Nouns ending in *s, ch, sh*, or *x*, add *es* to the singular; as, *fox, foxes; wish, wishes; glass, glasses; coach, coaches*.

3. Nouns ending in *y* preceded by a vowel (*a, e, i, o, u*) add *s*; as, *valley, valleys*, (*soliloquy, soliloquies* and *colloquy, colloquies* are exceptions). When *y* is preceded by a consonant (any letter other than a vowel), *y* is changed to *i* and *es* is added; as, *army, armies; pony, ponies; sty, sties*.

4. Most nouns ending in *f* or *fe* add *s*, as, *scarf, scarfs; safe, safes*. A few change *f* or *fe* to *v* and add *es*; as, *wife, wives; self, selves*. The others are: *beef, calf, elf, half, leaf, loaf, sheaf, shelf, staff, thief, wharf, wolf, life*. (*Wharf* has also a plural, *wharfs*.)

5. Most nouns ending in *o* add *s*; as, *cameo, cameos*. A number of nouns ending in *o* preceded by a consonant add *es*; as, *volcano, volcanoes*. The most important of the latter class are: *buffalo, cargo, calico, echo, embargo, flamingo, hero, motto, mulatto, negro, potato, tomato, tornado, torpedo, veto*.

6. Letters, figures, characters, etc., add the apostrophe and *s* (*'s*); as, *6's, c's, t's, that's.*

7. The following common words always form their plurals in an irregular way; as, *man, men; ox, oxen; goose, geese; woman, women; foot, feet; mouse, mice; child, children; tooth, teeth; louse, lice.*

Compound Nouns are those formed by the union of two words, either two nouns or a noun joined to some descriptive word or phrase.

8. The principal noun of a compound noun, whether it precedes or follows the descriptive part, is in most cases the noun that changes in forming the plural; as, *mothers-in-law, knights-errant, mouse-traps.* In a few compound words, both parts take a plural form; as, *man-servant, men-servants; knight-templar, knights-templars.*

9. Proper names and titles generally form plurals in the same way as do other nouns; as, *Senators Webster and Clay, the three Henrys.* Abbreviations of titles are little used in the plural, except *Messrs.* (*Mr.*), and *Drs.* (*Dr.*).

10. In forming the plurals of proper names where a title is used, either the title or the name may be put in the plural form. Sometimes both are made plural; as, *Miss Brown, the Misses Brown, the Miss Browns, the two Mrs. Browns.*

11. Some nouns are the same in both the singular and the plural; as, *deer, series, means, gross,* etc.

12. Some nouns used in two senses have two plural forms. The most important are the following:

brother	*brothers* (by blood)	*brethren* (by association)
cloth	*cloths* (kinds of cloth)	*clothes* (garments)
die	*dies* (for coinage)	*dice* (for games)
fish	*fishes* (separately)	*fish* (collectively)
genius	*geniuses* (men of genius)	*genii* (imaginary beings)
head	*heads* (of the body)	*head* (of cattle)
index	*indexes* (of books)	*indices* (in algebra)
pea	*peas* (separately)	*pease* (collectively)
penny	*pennies* (separately)	*pence* (collectively)
sail	*sails* (pieces of canvas)	*sail* (number of vessels)

shot   *shots* (number of discharges)   *shot* (number of balls)

13. Nouns from foreign languages frequently retain in the plural the form that they have in the language from which they are taken; as, *focus, foci; terminus, termini; alumnus, alumni; datum, data; stratum, strata; formula, formulæ; vortex, vortices; appendix, appendices; crisis, crises; oasis, oases; axis, axes; phenomenon, phenomena; automaton, automata; analysis, analyses; hypothesis, hypotheses; medium, media; vertebra, vertebræ; ellipsis, ellipses; genus, genera; fungus, fungi; minimum, minima; thesis, theses.*

EXERCISE 3

Write the plural, if any, of every singular noun in the following list; and the singular, if any, of every plural noun. Note those having no singular and those having no plural.

News, goods, thanks, scissors, proceeds, puppy, studio, survey, attorney, arch, belief, chief, charity, half, hero, negro, majority, Mary, vortex, memento, joy, lily, knight-templar, knight-errant, why, 4, x, son-in-law, Miss Smith, Mr. Anderson, country-man, hanger-on, major-general, oxen, geese, man-servant, brethren, strata, sheep, mathematics, pride, money, pea, head, piano, veto, knives, ratios, alumni, feet, wolves, president, sailor-boy, spoonful, rope-ladder, grandmother, attorney-general, cupful, go-between.

When in doubt respecting the form of any of the above, consult an unabridged dictionary.

14. Case. There are three cases in English: the Nominative, the Possessive, and the Objective.

The **Nominative Case;** the form used in address and as the subject of a verb.

The **Objective Case;** the form used as the object of a verb or a preposition. It is always the same in form as is the nominative.

Since no error in grammar can arise in the use of the nominative or the objective cases of nouns, no further discussion of these cases is here needed.

The **Possessive Case;** the form used to show ownership. In the forming of this case we have inflection.

15. The following are the rules for the forming of the possessive case:

1. Most nouns form the possessive by adding the apostrophe and *s* ('*s*); as, *man, man's; men, men's; pupil, pupil's; John, John's.*

2. Plural nouns ending in *s* form the possessive by adding only the apostrophe ('); as, *persons, persons'; writers, writers'*. In stating possession in the plural, then one should say: *Carpenters' tools sharpened here, Odd Fellows' wives are invited*, etc.

3. Some singular nouns ending in an *s* sound form the possessive by adding the apostrophe alone; as, *for appearance' sake, for goodness' sake*. But usage inclines to the adding of the apostrophe and *s* (*'s*) even if the singular noun does end in an *s* sound; as, *Charles's book, Frances's dress, the mistress's dress*.

4. When a compound noun, or a group of words treated as one name, is used to denote possession, the sign of the possessive is added to the last word only; as, *Charles and John's mother* (the mother of both Charles and John), *Brown and Smith's store* (the store of the firm Brown & Smith).

5. Where the succession of possessives is unpleasant or confusing, the substitution of a prepositional phrase should be made; as, *the house of the mother of Charles's partner*, instead of, *Charles's partner's mother's house*.

6. The sign of the possessive should be used with the word immediately preceding the word naming the thing possessed; as, *Father and mother's house, Smith, the lawyer's, office, The Senator from Utah's seat*.

7. Generally, nouns representing inanimate objects should not be used in the possessive case. It is better to say *the hands of the clock* than *the clock's hands*.

NOTE.—One should say *somebody else's*, not *somebody's else*. The expression *somebody else* always occurs in the one form, and in such cases the sign of the possessive should be added to the last word. Similarly, say, *no one else's, everybody else's*, etc.

EXERCISE 4

Write the possessives of the following:

Oxen, ox, brother-in-law, Miss Jones, goose, man, men, men-servants, man-servant, Maine, dogs, attorneys-at-law, Jackson & Jones, John the student, my friend John, coat, shoe, boy, boys, Mayor of Cleveland.

EXERCISE 5

Write sentences illustrating the use of the possessives you have formed for the first ten words under Exercise 4.

EXERCISE 6

Change the following expressions from the prepositional phrase form to the possessive:

1. The ships of Germany and France.
2. The garden of his mother and sister.
3. The credit of Jackson & Jones.
4. The signature of the president of the firm.

5. The coming of my grandfather.
6. The lives of our friends.
7. The dog of both John and William.
8. The dog of John and the dog of William.
9. The act of anybody else.
10. The shortcomings of Alice.
11. The poems of Robert Burns.
12. The wives of Henry the Eighth.
13. The home of Mary and Martha.
14. The novels of Dickens and the novels of Scott.
15. The farm of my mother and of my father.
16. The recommendation of Superintendent Norris.

EXERCISE 7

Correct such of the following expressions as need correction. If apostrophes are omitted, insert them in the proper places:

1. He walked to the precipices edge.
2. Both John and William's books were lost.
3. They sell boy's hats and mens' coats.
4. My friends' umbrella was stolen.
5. I shall buy a hat at Wanamaker's & Brown's.
6. This student's lessons.
7. These students books.
8. My daughters coming.
9. John's wife's cousin.
10. My son's wife's aunt.
11. Five years imprisonment under Texas's law.
12. John's books and Williams.
13. The Democrat's and Republican Convention.
14. France's and England's interests differ widely.
15. The moons' face was hidden.

16. Wine is made from the grape's juice.

17. Morton, the principals, signature.

18. Jones & Smith, the lawyers, office.

16. Gender. Gender in grammar is the quality of nouns or pronouns that denotes the sex of the person or thing represented. Those nouns or pronouns meaning males are in the **Masculine Gender**. Those meaning females are in the **Feminine Gender**. Those referring to things without sex are in the **Neuter Gender**.

In nouns gender is of little consequence. The only regular inflection is the addition of the syllable-*ess* to certain masculine nouns to denote the change to the feminine gender; as, *author, authoress; poet, poetess*. -I*x* is also sometimes added for the same purpose; as, *administrator, administratrix*.

The feminine forms were formerly much used, but their use is now being discontinued, and the noun of masculine gender used to designate both sexes.

CHAPTER III

PRONOUNS

17. Pronoun and Antecedent. A **Pronoun** is a word used instead of a noun. The noun in whose stead it stands is called its **Antecedent**. *John took Mary's **book** and gave **it** to **his** friend.* In this sentence *book* is the antecedent of the pronoun *it*, and *John* is the antecedent of *his*.

18. Pronouns should agree with their antecedents in person, gender, and number.

19. Personal Pronouns are those that by their form indicate the speaker, the person spoken to, or the person or thing spoken about.

Pronouns of the **First Person** indicate the speaker; they are: *I, me, my, mine, we, us, our, ours*.

Pronouns of the **Second Person** indicate the person or thing spoken to; they are: *you, your, yours*. There are also the grave or solemn forms in the second person, which are now little used; these are: *thou, thee, thy, thine*, and *ye*.

Pronouns of the **Third Person** indicate the person or thing spoken of; they are: *he, his, him, she, her, hers, they, their, theirs, them, it, its*.

Few errors are made in the use of the proper person of the pronoun.

20. Gender of Pronouns. The following pronouns indicate sex or gender; Masculine: *he, his, him*. Feminine: *she, her, hers*. Neuter: *it, its*.

In order to secure agreement in gender it is necessary to know the gender of the noun, expressed or understood, to which the pronoun refers. Gender of nouns is important only so far as it concerns the use of pronouns. Study carefully the following rules in regard to gender. These rules apply to the singular number only, since all plurals of whatever gender are referred to by *they, their, theirs*, etc.

The following rules govern the gender of pronouns:

Masculine; referred to by ***he, his***, and ***him***:

1. Nouns denoting males are always masculine.

2. Nouns denoting things remarkable for strength, power, sublimity, or size, when those things are regarded as if they were persons, are masculine; *as*, **Winter**, *with **his** chilly army, destroyed them all*.

3. Singular nouns denoting persons of both sexes are masculine; as, *Every one* brought ***his*** *umbrella.*

Feminine; referred to by ***she, her***, or ***hers***:

1. Nouns denoting females are always feminine.

2. Nouns denoting objects remarkable for beauty, gentleness, and peace, when spoken of as if they were persons, are feminine; as, ***Sleep*** *healed him with* ***her*** *fostering care.*

Neuter; referred to by ***it*** and ***its***:

1. Nouns denoting objects without sex are neuter.

2. Nouns denoting objects whose sex is disregarded are neuter; as, *It is a pretty child, The* ***wolf*** *is the most savage of* ***its*** *race.*

3. Collective nouns referring to a group of individuals as a unit are neuter; as, *The* ***jury*** *gives its* ***verdict***, *The* ***committee*** *makes* ***its*** *report.*

An animal named may be regarded as masculine; feminine, or neuter, according to the characteristics the writer fancies it to possess; as, *The* ***wolf*** *seeks* ***his*** *prey, The* ***mouse*** *nibbled* ***her*** *way into the box, The* ***bird*** *seeks* ***its*** *nest.*

Certain nouns may be applied to persons of either sex. They are then said to be of **Common Gender.** There are no pronouns of common gender; hence those nouns are referred to as follows:

1. By masculine pronouns when known to denote males; as, ***My class-mate*** (known to be Harry) *is taking* ***his*** *examinations.*

2. By feminine pronouns when known to denote females; as, ***Each of the pupils*** *of the Girls High School brought* ***her*** *book.*

3. By masculine pronouns when there is nothing in the connection of the thought to show the sex of the object; as, *Let every* ***person*** *bring his book.*

21. Number of Pronouns. A more common source of error than disagreement in gender is disagreement in number. *They, their, theirs,* and *them* are plural, but are often improperly used when only singular pronouns should be used. The cause of the error is failure to realize the true antecedent.

If ***anybody*** *makes that statement,* ***they*** *are misinformed.* This sentence is wrong. *Anybody* refers to only one person; both *any* and *body*, the parts of the word, denote the singular. The sentence should read, *If* ***anybody*** *makes that statement,* ***he*** *is misinformed.* Similarly, *Let* ***everybody*** *keep* ***their*** *peace*, should read, *Let* ***everybody*** *keep* ***his*** *peace.*

22. Compound Antecedents. Two or more antecedents connected by *or* or *nor* are frequently referred to by the plural when the singular should be used. *Neither John nor James brought **their** books*, should read, *Neither John nor James brought **his** books*. When a pronoun has two or more singular antecedents connected by *or* or *nor*, the pronoun must be in the singular number; but if one of the antecedents is plural, the pronoun must, also, be in the plural; as, *Neither the Mormon nor his wives denied **their** religion*.

When a pronoun has two or more antecedents connected by *and*, the pronoun must be in the plural number; as, *John and James brought **their** books*.

Further treatment of number will be given under verbs.

EXERCISE 8

Fill in the blanks in the following sentences with the proper pronouns. See that there is agreement in person, gender, and number:

1. Has everybody finished —— work.
2. If any one wishes a longer time, let —— hold up —— hand.
3. The panther sprang from —— lurking place.
4. Many a man has (have) lost —— money in speculation.
5. The cat came each day for —— bit of meat.
6. Everyone has to prove —— right to a seat.
7. Let every boy answer for —— self (selves).
8. The crowd was so great that we could hardly get through ——.
9. Let any boy guess this riddle if —— can.
10. Company H was greatly reduced in —— numbers.
11. Every animal has some weapon with which —— can defend ——self (selves).
12. Nowhere does each dare do as —— pleases (please).
13. The elephant placed —— great foot on the man's chest.
14. The child did not know —— mother.
15. Death gathers —— unfailing harvest.
16. Every kind of animal has —— natural enemies.

17. The committee instructed —— chairman to report the matter.

18. Two men were present, but neither would tell what —— saw.

19. Truth always triumphs over —— enemies.

20. Nobody did —— duty more readily than I.

21. The cat never fails to catch —— prey.

22. I have used both blue crayon and red crayon, but —— does (do) not write so clearly as white.

23. If John and Henry whisper (whispers) —— will be punished.

24. If John or Henry whisper (whispers) —— will be punished.

25. Both Columbus and Cabot failed to realize the importance of —— discoveries.

26. Neither the lawyer nor the sheriff liked —— task.

27. The canary longed to escape from —— cage.

28. The rat ran to —— hole.

29. The dog seemed to know —— master was dead.

30. Everyone should try to gather a host of friends about ——.

31. If any one wishes to see me, send —— to the Pierce Building.

32. Probably everybody is discouraged at least once in —— life.

33. Nobody should deceive ——selves (self).

34. Let each take —— own seat.

35. Let each girl in the class bring —— book.

36. Let each bring —— book.

37. Let each bring —— sewing.

38. The fox dropped —— meat in the pool.

39. The rock lay on —— side.

40. Let sleep enter with —— healing touch.

41. Each believed that —— had been elected a delegate to the Mother's Congress.

42. Consumption demands each year —— thousands of victims.

43. Summer arrays ——self (selves) with flowers.

44. Despair seized him in —— powerful grasp.

45. If any boy or any girl finds the book, let —— bring it to me.

46. Let every man and every woman speak ——mind.

47. Spring set forth —— beauties.

48. How does the mouse save —— self (selves) from being caught?

49. The hen cackled —— loudest.

50. Some man or boy lost —— hat.

51. John or James will favor us with —— company.

52. Neither the captain nor the soldiers showed ——self (selves) during the fight.

53. If the boys or their father come we shall be glad to see ——.

54. Every man and every boy received —— dinner.

55. Every man or boy gave —— offering.

EXERCISE 9

By what gender of the pronouns would you refer to the following nouns?

Snake, death, care, mercy, fox, bear, walrus, child, baby, friend (uncertain sex), friend (known to be Mary), everybody, someone, artist, flower, moon, sun, sorrow, fate, student, foreigner, Harvard University, earth, Germany?

23. Relative Pronouns. Relative Pronouns are pronouns used to introduce adjective or noun clauses that are not interrogative. In the sentence, *The man **that I mentioned** has come*, the relative clause, *that I mentioned*, is an adjective clause modifying *man*. In the sentence, ***Whom she means**, I do not know*, the relative clause is, *whom she means*, and is a noun clause forming the object of the verb *know*.

The relative pronouns are *who* (*whose, whom*), *which, that* and *what*. But *and* and *as* are sometimes relative pronouns. There are, also, compound relative pronouns, which will be mentioned later.

24. *Who* (with its possessive and objective forms, *whose* and *whom*) should be used when the antecedent denotes persons. When the antecedent denotes things or animals, *which* should be used. *That* may be used with antecedents denoting persons, animals or things, and is the proper relative to use when the antecedent includes both persons and things. *What*, when used as a relative, seldom properly refers to persons. It always introduces a substantive clause, and is equivalent to *that which*; as, *It is **what** (that which) he wants*.

25. *That* is known as the **Restrictive Relative**, because it should be used whenever the relative clause limits the substantive, unless *who* or *which* is of more pleasing sound in the sentence. In the sentence, *He is the man **that did the act***, the relative clause, *that did the act*, defines what is meant by man; without the relative clause the sentence clearly would be incomplete. Similarly, in the sentence, *The book **that I want** is that red-backed history*, the restrictive relative clause is, *that I want*, and limits the application of *book*.

26. *Who* and *which* are known as the **Explanatory** or **Non-Restrictive Relatives**, and should be used ordinarily only to introduce relative clauses which add some new thought to the author's principal thought. *Spanish, **which is the least complex language**, is the easiest to learn*. In this sentence the principal thought is, *Spanish is the easiest language to learn*. The relative clause, *which is the least complex language*, is a thought, which, though not fully so important as the principal thought, is more nearly coördinate than subordinate in its value. It adds an additional thought of the speaker explaining the character of the Spanish language. When *who* and *which* are thus used as explanatory relatives, we see that the relative clause may be omitted without making the sentence incomplete.

Compare the following sentences:

Explanatory relative clause: That book, *which is about history*, has a red cover.

Restrictive relative clause: The book *that is about history* has a red cover.

Explanatory relative clause: Lincoln, *who was one of the world's greatest men*, was killed by Booth.

Restrictive relative clause: The Lincoln *that was killed by Booth* was one of the world's greatest men.

NOTE.—See §111, for rule as to the punctuation of relative clauses.

27. Interrogative Pronouns. An Interrogative Pronoun is a pronoun used to ask a question. The interrogative pronouns are, *who* (*whose*, *whom*), *which*, and *what*. In respect to antecedents, *who* should be used only in reference to persons; *which* and *what* may be used with any antecedent, persons, animals, or things.

EXERCISE 10

Choose the proper relative or interrogative pronoun to be inserted in each of the following sentences. Insert commas where they are needed. (See **§111**):

1. The kindly physician ——— was so greatly loved is dead.

2. This is the man ——— all are praising.

3. John ——— is my coachman is sick.

4. The intelligence ——— he displayed was remarkable.

5. Intelligence ——— he had hitherto not manifested now showed its presence.

6. He maintains that the book ——— you used is now ruined. (Does *which* or *that* have the more pleasing sound here?)

7. The pleasure ——— education gives the man ——— has it is a sufficient reward for the trouble ——— it has cost.

8. That man ——— wears a cap is a foreigner.

9. The best hotel is the one ——— is nearest the station.

10. Who is it ——— is worthy of that honor?

11. The carriages and the drivers ——— you ordered yesterday have arrived.

12. ——— thing is it ——— you want?

13. He purchased ——— he wished.

14. There is no cloud ——— has not its silver lining.

15. It is the same dog ——— I bought.

16. The man and horse ——— you see pass here every afternoon.

17. ——— did they seek?

18. They inquired ——— he was going to do.

19. Who was it ——— lost the book?

20. The man —— was a Frenchman was very much excited.

21. It is neither the party nor its candidate —— gains support.

22. That is a characteristic —— makes him seem almost rude.

23. It is the same tool —— I used all day.

24. He is a man —— inspires little confidence.

25. —— does he expect of us?

26. It is just such a thing —— I need.

27. There are few —— will vote for him.

28. The wagon and children —— you just saw came from our town.

29. He —— writes out his lesson does all —— can be expected.

30. Was it you or the cat —— made that noise?

31. It is the same song —— he always sings.

32. Such —— I have is yours.

33. All the men and horses —— we had were lost.

34. That is —— pleased me most and —— everyone talked about.

35. The horse was one —— I had never ridden before.

36. That is —— everyone said.

28. Case Forms of Pronouns. Some personal, relative, and interrogative pronouns have distinctive forms for the different cases, and the failure to use the proper case forms in the sentence is one of the most frequent sources of error. The case to be used is to be determined by the use which the pronoun, not its antecedent, has in the sentence. In the sentence, *I name him*, note that *him* is the object of the verb *name*. In the sentence, **Whom** *do you seek*, although coming at the first of the sentence, *whom* is grammatically the object of the verb *seek*. In the use of pronouns comes the most important need for a knowledge of when to use the different cases.

Note the following different case forms of pronouns:

Nominative: *I, we, you, thou, ye, he, she, they, it, who.*

Objective: *me, us, you, thee, ye, him, her, it, them, whom.*

Possessive: *my, mine, our, ours, thy, thine, your, yours, his, her, hers, its, their, theirs, whose.*

It will be noted that, while some forms are the same in both the nominative and objective cases, *I, we, he, she, they, thou,* and *who* **are only proper where the nominative case should be used.** *Me, us, him, them, thee, whom,* and *her*, except when *her* is possessive, **are only proper when the objective case is demanded.** These forms must be remembered. It is only with these pronouns that mistakes are made in the use of the nominative and objective cases.

29. The following outline explains the use of the different case forms of the pronouns. The outline should be mastered.

The Nominative Case should be used:

1. When the noun or pronoun is the subject of a finite verb; that is, a verb other than an infinitive. See 3 under Objective Case.

2. When it is an attribute complement. An attribute complement, as explained in Chapter I, is a word used in the predicate explaining or stating something about the subject. Examples: *It is **I**, The man was **he**, The people were **they** of whom we spoke.*

3. When it is used without relation to any other part of speech, as in direct address or exclamation.

The Objective Case should be used:

1. When the noun or pronoun is the object of a verb; as, *He named **me**, She deceived **them**, They watch **us**.*

2. When it is the object of a preposition, expressed or understood: as, *He spoke of **me**, For **whom** do you take me, He told (to) **me** a story.*

3. When it is the subject of an infinitive; as, *I told **him** to go, I desire **her** to hope.* The infinitives are the parts of the verb preceded by *to*; as, *to go, to see, to be, to have been seen*, etc. The sign of the infinitive, to, is not always expressed. The objective case is, nevertheless, used; as, *Let **him** (to) go, Have **her** (to be) told about it.*

4. When it is an attribute complement of an expressed subject of the infinitive *to be*; as, *They believed her to be **me**, He denied it to have been him.* (See Note 2 below.)

The Possessive Case should be used:

When the word is used as a possessive modifier; as, *They spoke of **her** being present, The book is **his** (book), It is **their** fault.*

NOTE 1.—When a substantive is placed by the side of another substantive and is used to explain it, it is said to be in **Apposition** with that other substantive and takes the case of that word; as, *It* was given *to John Smith,* **him** *whom you see there.*

NOTE 2.—The attribute complement should always have the case of that subject of the verb which is expressed in the sentence. Thus, in the sentence, *I could not wish John to be* **him**, *him* is properly in the objective case, since there is an expressed subject of the infinitive, *John*, which is in the objective case. But in the sentence, *I should hate to be* **he**, *he* is properly in the nominative case, since the only subject that is expressed in the sentence is *I*, in the nominative case.

NOTE 3.—Where the relative pronoun *who (whom)* is the subject of a clause that itself is the object clause of a verb or a preposition, it is always in the nominative case. Thus the following sentences are both correct: *I delivered it to* **who** *owned it, Bring home* **whoever** *will come with you.*

EXERCISE 11

Write sentences illustrating the correct use of each of the following pronouns:

I, whom, who, we, me, us, they, whose, theirs, them, she, him, he, its, mine, our, thee, thou.

EXERCISE 12

In the following sentences choose the proper form from the words in italics:

1. My brother and *I me* drove to the east end of the town.
2. Between you and *I me* things are doubtful.
3. May James and *I me* go to the circus?
4. Will you permit James and *I me* to go to the play?
5. Who made that noise? Only *I me*.
6. He introduced us all, *I me* among the rest.
7. He promised to bring candy to Helen and *I me*.
8. Was it *I me* that you asked for?
9. Who spoke? *I me*.
10. I am taken to be *he him*.
11. No, it could not have been *me I*.
12. All have gone but you and *I me*.

13. You suffer more than *me I*.

14. Everyone has failed in the examination except you and *I me*.

15. He asked you and *I me* to come to his office.

16. See if there is any mail for Mary and *me I*.

17. Neither you nor *I me* can teach the class.

18. They think it to be *I me*.

19. This is the student *whom who* all are praising.

20. The one that is *he him* wears a brown hat.

21. He is a man *who whom* all admired.

22. He is one of those men *who whom* we call snobs.

23. I did not see that it was *her she*.

24. It is in fact *he him*.

25. He still believes it to be *them they*.

26. Between you and *I me*, it is my opinion that *him he* and John will disagree.

27. We saw John and *she her*; we know it was *them they*.

28. I did not speak of either you or *she her*.

29. Our cousins and *we us* are going to the Art Gallery.

30. Aunt Mary has asked our cousins and *us we* to take dinner at her house.

31. They are more eager than *we us* since they have not seen her for a long time.

32. It could not have been *we us who whom* you suspected.

33. *We us* boys are going to the ball game.

34. They sent letters to all *who whom* they thought would contribute.

35. This money was given by John *who whom* you know is very stingy.

36. The superintendent, *who whom*, I cannot doubt, is responsible

37. for this error, must be discharged.

38. The teacher told you and *I me* to stay.

39. The teacher told you and *him he* to stay.

40. The teacher told you and *she her* to stay.

41. There are many miles between England and *we us*.

42. They can't play the game better than *we us*.

43. It is unpleasant for such as *they them* to witness such things.

44. Between a teacher and *he him who whom* he teaches there is sometimes a strong fellowship.

45. You are nearly as strong as *him he*.

46. All were present but John and *he him*.

47. Father believed it was *she her*.

48. Mother knew it to be *her she*.

49. It was either *he him* or *she her* that called.

50. Because of *his him* being young, they tried to shield him.

51. It was *he him who whom* the manager said ought to be promoted.

52. The throne was held by a king *who whom* historians believe to have been insane.

53. *Who whom* did he say the man was?

54. *Who whom* did he say the judge suspected?

55. *Who whom* do you consider to be the brightest man?

56. *Who whom* do you think is the brightest man?

57. He cannot learn from such as *thou thee*.

58. If they only rob such as *thou thee*, they are honest.

59. What dost *thou thee* know?

60. They do tell *thee thou* the truth.

61. She told John and *me I* to study.

62. My father allowed my brother and *her she* to go.

63. My brother and *she her* were allowed to go by my father.

64. Turn not away from *him he* that is needy.

65. Neither Frances nor *she her* was at fault.

66. The property goes to *they them*.

67. He thought it was *her she*, but it was *him he* and William who did it.

68. It was through *she her* that word came to *me I*.

69. I thought it was *her she*.

70. I wish you were more like *he him*.

71. I thought it to be *she her*.

72. It seems to be *he*. I should hate to be *he*. I should like to be *he* or *she*. (All these sentences are in the correct form.)

73. He is a man in *whom who* I have little faith.

74. You are as skillful as *she her*.

75. We escorted her mother and *her she* to the station.

76. *She her* and *I me* are going on the boat.

77. If any are late it will not be *us we*.

78. *Who whom* are you going to collect it from?

79. *Who whom* do men say that he is?

80. *Who whom* do you think *him he* to be?

81. *They them* and their children have gone abroad.

82. It was not *they them*.

83. *Who whom* am I said to be?

84. I do not know to *who whom* to direct him.

85. How can one tell *who whom* is at home now?

86. *Who whom* is that for?

87. Choose *who whom* you please.

88. Do you think *I me* to be *her she who whom* you call Kate?

89. Some *who whom* their friends expected were kept away.

90. Give it to *who whom* seems to want it most.

91. *Who whom* do you think I saw there?

92. I hope it was *she her who whom* we saw.

93. It could not have been *him he*.
94. *Who whom* did you say did it?
95. Let *them they* come at once.
96. The man on *who whom* I relied was absent.
97. I know it was *they them who whom* did it.
98. Will he let *us we* go?
99. It came from *they them who whom* should not have sent it.
100. It was not *us we* from *who whom* it came.
101. Can it be *she her*?
102. *Thou thee* art mistaken.
103. Let me tell *thee thou, thee thou* wilt do wrong.
104. Send *who whom* wants the pass to me.
105. Tell *who whom* you choose to come.
106. Is he the man for *who whom* the city is named?
107. The book is for *who whom* needs it.
108. I do not know *who whom* the book is for.

30. The **Compound Personal Pronouns** are formed by adding *self* or *selves* to certain of the objective and possessive personal pronouns; as, *herself, myself, itself, themselves*, etc. They are used to add emphasis to an expression; as, I, **myself**, did it, He, **himself**, said so. They are also used reflexively after verbs and prepositions; as, He mentioned **himself**, He did it for **himself**.

The compound personal pronouns should generally be confined to their emphatic and reflexive use. Do not say, **Myself** and John will come, but, John and **I** will come. Do not say, They invited John and **myself**, but, They invited John and **me**.

The compound personal pronouns have no possessive forms; but for the sake of emphasis *own* with the ordinary possessive form is used; as, I have my **own** book, Bring your **own** work, He has a home of his **own**.

31. There are no such forms as *hisself, your'n, his'n, her'n, theirself, theirselves, their'n*. In place of these use simply *his, her, their,* or *your*.

EXERCISE 13

Write sentences illustrating the correct use of the following simple and compound personal pronouns:

Myself, me, I, them, themselves, him, himself, her, herself, itself, our, ourselves.

EXERCISE 14

Choose the correct form in the following sentences. Punctuate properly. (See §108):

1. *Yourself you* and John were mentioned
2. She told Mary and *me myself* to go with *her herself.*
3. The book is for *you yourself* and *I me myself.*
4. Henry and *I me myself* are in the same class.
5. He thinks *you yourself* and *I me myself* should bring the books.
6. Our friends and *we us ourselves* are going out to-night.
7. *Herself she* and her husband have been sick.
8. *They themselves* and their children have gone abroad.
9. You play the violin better than *he himself.*
10. The machine failed to work well, because *it itself* and the engine were not properly adjusted to each other.
11. Let them do it *theirselves themselves.*
12. He came by *hisself himself.*
13. The teacher *hisself himself* could not have done better.
14. I'll bring my gun, and you bring *your'n yours your* own.
15. That book is *his'n his.*

EXERCISE 15

Fill the blanks in the following sentences with the proper emphatic or reflexive forms. Punctuate properly. (See §108):

1. He —— said so.
2. I —— will do it.
3. We —— will look after her.
4. That, I tell you, is —— book.
5. It belongs to me ——.

6. Those books are my ——.
7. Let them —— pay for it.
8. The horse is to be for —— use.
9. The horse is to be for the use of ——.
10. He said it to ——.
11. He deceived ——.
12. I do not wish —— to be prominent.

32. The **Compound Relative Pronouns** are formed by adding *ever, so,* or *soever* to the relative pronouns, *who, which,* and *what;* as, *whoever, whatever, whomever, whosoever, whoso, whosoever,* etc. It will be noted that *whoever, whosoever,* and *whoso* have objective forms, *whomever, whomsoever,* and *whomso;* and possessive forms, *whosoever, whosesoever,* and *whoseso.* These forms must be used whenever the objective or possessive case is demanded. Thus, one should say, *I will give it to **whomever** I find there.* (See §29 and Note 3.)

EXERCISE 16

Fill the following blanks with the proper forms of the compound relatives:

1. We will refer the question to —— you may name.
2. —— it may have been, it was not he.
3. I shall receive presents from —— I wish.
4. It was between him and —— was with him.
5. —— they may choose, I will not vote for him.
6. Let them name —— they think will win.
7. Give it to —— you think needs it most.
8. He may take —— he cares to.
9. He will take —— property he finds there.
10. He promised to ask the question of —— he found there.
11. —— can have done it?
12. —— else may be said, that is not true.
13. There are the two chairs; you may take —— you like.
14. —— you take will suit me.
15. You may have —— you wish.

16. —— is nominated, will you vote for him?

17. —— they nominate, I will vote for him.

18. —— does that is a partizan.

19. —— candidate is elected, I will be satisfied.

20. He may name —— he thinks best.

21. —— he says is worthy of attention.

22. —— she takes after, she is honest.

23. —— follows him will be sorry.

24. —— he may be, he is no gentleman.

25. —— they do is praised.

33. There are certain words, called **Adjective Pronouns**, which are regarded as pronouns, because, although they are properly adjective in their meaning, the nouns which they modify are never expressed; as, *One* (there is a possessive form, *one's*, and a plural form, *ones*), *none, this, that, these, those, other, former, some, few, many*, etc.

34. Some miscellaneous cautions in the use of pronouns:

1. The pronoun *I* should always be capitalized, and should, when used as part of a compound subject, be placed second; as, *James and I were present,* not *I and James were present.*

2. Do not use the common and grave forms of the personal pronouns in the same sentence; as, ***Thou*** *wilt do this whether* ***you*** *wish or not.*

3. Avoid the use of personal pronouns where they are unnecessary; as, *John,* ***he*** *did it, or Mary,* ***she*** *said.* This is a frequent error in speech.

4. Let the antecedent of each pronoun be clearly apparent. Note the uncertainty in the following sentence; *He sent a box of cheese, and* ***it*** *was made of wood.* The antecedent of *it* is not clear. Again, *A man told his son to take* ***his*** *coat home.* The antecedent of *his* is very uncertain. Such errors are frequent.

In relative clauses this error may sometimes be avoided by placing the relative clause as near as possible to the noun it limits. Note the following sentence: *A cat was found in the* ***yard which*** *wore a blue ribbon.* The grammatical inference would be that the yard wore the blue ribbon. The sentence might be changed to, *A* ***cat, which*** *wore a blue ribbon, was found in the yard.*

5. Relative clauses referring to the same thing require the same relative pronoun to introduce them; as, *The book **that** we found and the book **that** he lost are the same.*

6. Use *but that* when *but* is a conjunction and *that* introduces a noun clause; as, *There is no doubt **but that** he will go.* Use *but what* when *but* is a preposition in the sense of *except*; as, *He has no money but (except) **what** I gave him.*

7. *Them* is a pronoun and should never be used as an adjective. *Those* is the adjective which should be used in its place; as, *Those people*, not, *Them people.*

8. Avoid using *you* and *they* indefinitely; as, ***You*** *seldom hear of such things,* ***They*** *make chairs there.* Instead, say, ***One*** *seldom hears of such things, Chairs are made there.*

9. *Which* should not be used with a clause or phrase as its antecedent. Both the following sentences are wrong: *He sent me to see John,* ***which*** *I did. Their whispering became very loud, which annoyed the preacher.*

10. Never use an apostrophe with the possessive pronouns, *its, yours, theirs, ours* and *hers*.

EXERCISE 17

Correct the following sentences so that they do not violate the cautions above stated:

1. How can you say that when thou knowest better?
2. May I and Mary go to the concert?
3. He asked me to write to him, which I did.
4. Grant thou to us your blessing.
5. The train it was twenty minutes late.
6. Mother she said I might go.
7. Mary told her mother she was mistaken.
8. The man cannot leave his friend, for if he should leave him he would be angry.
9. Sarah asked her aunt how old she was.
10. That is the man whom we named and that did it.
11. Mr. Jones went to Mr. Smith and told him that his dog was lost.
12. This is the book that we found and which he lost.

13.   She told her sister that if she could not get to the city, she thought she had better go home.

14.   Jack cannot see Henry because he is so short.

15.   Then Jack and George, they went home.

16.   Bring them books here.

17.   Them are all wrong.

18.   There are no men in the room but that can be bought.

19.   I have no doubt but what it was done.

20.   Them there should be corrected.

21.   I have faith in everything but that he says.

22.   I have no fears but what it can be done.

23.   Napoleon, he threw his armies across the Rhine.

24.   Thou knowest not what you are doing.

25.   It was thought advisable to exile Napoleon, which was done.

26.   A grapevine had grown along the fence which was full of grapes.

27.   Keep them people out of here.

28.   The two cars contained horses that were painted yellow.

29.   She is a girl who is always smiling and that all like.

30.   You never can tell about foreigners.

31.   They say that is not true.

32.   The cabin needed to be swept, which we did.

33.   They use those methods in some schools.

34.   It is the house that is on the corner and which is painted white.

35.   You can easily learn history if you have a good memory.

36.   How can you tell but what it will rain?

37.   He does everything but what he should do.

38.   He has everything but that he needs.

39.   It was a collie dog which we had and that was stolen.

40. Aunt, she said that she didn't know but what she would go.
41. Tell I and John about it.
42. He went to his father and told him he had sinned.
43. Dost thou know what you doest?
44. It's appearance was deceitful.
45. The chair was also their's.
46. There is a slight difference between mine and your's.
47. Which of the two is her's?
48. They are both our's.

CHAPTER IV

ADJECTIVES AND ADVERBS

35. An **Adjective** is a word used to modify a noun or a pronoun. An **Adverb** is a word used to modify a verb, an adjective, or another adverb. Adjectives and adverbs are very closely related in both their forms and their use.

36. Comparison. The variation of adjectives and adverbs to indicate the degree of modification they express is called **Comparison**. There are three degrees of comparison.

The **Positive Degree** indicates the mere possession of a quality; as, *true, good, sweet, fast, lovely.*

The **Comparative Degree** indicates a stronger degree of the quality than the positive; as, *truer, sweeter, better, faster, lovelier.*

The **Superlative Degree** indicates the highest degree of quality; as, *truest, sweetest, best, fastest, loveliest.*

Where the adjectives and adverbs are compared by inflection they are said to be compared regularly. In regular comparison the comparative is formed by adding *er*, and the superlative by adding *est*. If the word ends in *y*, the *y* is changed to *i* before adding the ending; as, *pretty, prettier, prettiest.*

Where the adjectives and adverbs have two or more syllables, most of them are compared by the use of the adverbs *more* and *most*, or, if the comparison be a descending one, by the use of *less* and *least*; as, *beautiful, more beautiful, most beautiful,* and *less beautiful, least beautiful.*

37. Some adjectives and adverbs are compared by changing to entirely different words in the comparative and superlative. Note the following:

POSITIVE	COMPARATIVE	SUPERLATIVE
bad, ill, evil, badly	worse	worst
far	farther, further	farthest, furthest
forth	further	furthest
fore	former	foremost, first
good, well	better	best

hind	hinder	hindmost
late	later, latter	latest, last
little	less	least
much, many	more	most
old	older, elder	oldest, eldest

NOTE.—*Badly* and *forth* may be used only as adverbs. *Well* is usually an adverb; as, *He talks well*, but may be used as an adjective; as, *He seems well*.

38. Confusion of Adjectives and Adverbs. An adjective is often used where an adverb is required, and vice versa. The sentence, *She talks **foolish***, is wrong, because here the word to be modified is *talks*, and since *talks* is a verb, the adverb *foolishly* should be used. The sentence, *She looks **charmingly***, means, as it stands, that her manner of looking at a thing is charming. What is intended to be said is that she appears as if she was a charming woman. To convey that meaning, the adjective, *charming*, should have been used, and the sentence should read, *She looks charming*. Wherever the word modifies a verb or an adjective or another adverb, an adverb should be used, and wherever the word, whatever its location in the sentence, modifies a noun or pronoun, an adjective should be used.

39. The adjective and the adverb are sometimes alike in form. Thus, both the following sentences are correct: *He works **hard*** (adverb), and *His work is **hard*** (adjective). But, usually, where the adjective and the adverb correspond at all, the adverb has the additional ending *ly*; as, *The track is **smooth***, (adjective), and *The train runs **smoothly***, (adverb).

EXERCISE 18

In the following sentences choose from the italicized words the proper word to be used:

1. The sunset looks *beautiful beautifully*.
2. The man acted *strange strangely*.
3. Write *careful carefully* and speak *distinct distinctly*.
4. Speak *slow slowly*.
5. He acted *bad badly*.
6. He behaved very *proper properly*.
7. The boat runs *smooth smoothly*.
8. He is a *remarkable remarkably* poor writer.

9. I am in *extremely extreme* good health.
10. The typewriter works *good well*.
11. The bird warbles *sweet sweetly*.
12. He was *terrible terribly* angry.
13. He was in a *terrible terribly* dangerous place.
14. He talks *plainer more plainly* than he ever did before.
15. The dead Roman looked *fierce fiercely*.
16. The fire burns *brilliant brilliantly*.
17. You are *exceeding exceedingly* generous.
18. He struggled *manful manfully* against the opposition.
19. My health is *poor poorly*.
20. He is sure surely a *fine fellow*.
21. Have everything *suitable suitably* decorated.
22. That can be done *easy easily*.
23. I can speak *easier more easily* than I can write.
24. The music of the orchestra was *decided decidedly* poor.
25. She is a *remarkable remarkably* beautiful girl.
26. The wind roared *awful awfully*.
27. The roar of the wind was *awful awfully*.
28. I have studied grammar *previous previously* to this year.
29. I didn't study because I felt too *bad badly* to read.
30. The roses smell *sweetly sweet*.
31. They felt very *bad badly* at being beaten.
32. That violin sounds *different differently* from this one.
33. The soldiers fought *gallant gallantly*.
34. She looks *sweet sweetly* in that dress.
35. I can wear this coat *easy easily*.
36. Speak *gentle gently* to him.
37. He talks *warm warmly* on that subject.

38. He works *well good* and *steady steadily*.

39. He stood *thoughtful thoughtfully* for a moment and then went *quiet quietly* to his tent.

40. He walked down the street *slow slowly*, but all the time looked *eager eagerly* about him.

41. The music sounds *loud loudly*.

42. That coin rings *true truly*.

43. He looked *angry angrily* at his class.

44. He moved *silent silently* about in the crowd.

45. His coat fits *nice nicely*.

46. That is *easy easily* to do.

47. He went over the work very *thorough thoroughly*.

EXERCISE 19

The adjectives and adverbs in the following sentences are correctly used. In every case show what they modify:

1. The water lay smooth in the lake.
2. She looked cold.
3. The train runs smoothly now.
4. The sun shone bright at the horizon.
5. The sun shone brightly all day.
6. She looks coldly about her.
7. Be careful in your study of these sentences.
8. Study these sentences carefully.
9. We found the way easy.
10. We found the way easily.
11. He looked good.
12. He looked well.
13. We arrived safe.
14. We arrived safely.
15. Speak gently.

16. Let your speech be gentle.

EXERCISE 20

Write sentences containing the following words correctly used:

Thoughtful, thoughtfully, masterful, masterfully, hard, hardly, cool, coolly, rapid, rapidly, ungainly, careful, carefully, eager, eagerly, sweet, sweetly, gracious, graciously.

40. Improper Forms of Adjectives. The wrong forms in the following list of adjectives are frequently used in place of the right forms:

RIGHT	WRONG
everywhere	everywheres
not nearly	nowhere near
not at all	not much or not muchly
ill	illy
first	firstly
thus	thusly
much	muchly
unknown	unbeknown
complexioned	complected

EXERCISE 21

Correct the errors in the following sentences:

1. She goes everywheres.
2. Hers is the most illy behaved child I know.
3. Not muchly will I go.
4. Use the lesser quantity first.
5. He is nowhere near so bright as John.
6. You do the problem thusly.
7. The causes are firstly, ignorance, and second, lack of energy.
8. They came unbeknown to me.

9. He is a dark complected man.

10. It all happened unbeknownst to them.

11. His vote was nowhere near so large as usual.

41. Errors in comparison are frequently made. Observe carefully the following rules:

1. The superlative should not be used in comparing only two things. One should say, *He is the **larger** of the two*, not *He is the **largest** of the two*. But, *He is the largest of the three*, is right.

2. A comparison should not be attempted by adjectives that express absolute quality—adjectives that cannot be compared; as, *round, perfect, equally, universal*. A thing may be *round* or *perfect*, but it cannot be *more round* or *most round, more perfect* or *most perfect*.

3. When two objects are used in the comparative, one must not be included in the other; but, when two objects are used in the superlative, one must be included in the other. It is wrong to say, *The discovery of America was **more important than any** geographical discovery*, for that is saying that the discovery of America was more important than itself—an absurdity. But it would be right to say, *The discovery of America was more important **than any other** geographical discovery*. One should not say, *He is the most honest **of his** fellow-workmen*, for he is not one of his fellow-workmen. One should say, *He is more honest **than any** of his fellow-workmen*, or, *He is the most honest **of all** the workmen*. To say, *This machine is **better than any** machine*, is incorrect, but to say, *This machine is better **than any other** machine*, is correct. To say, *This machine is the **best of any** machine* (or *any other machine*), is wrong, because all machines are meant, not one machine or some machines. To say, *This machine is the **best of** machines* (or *the best of all machines*), is correct.

Note the following rules in regard to the use of *other* in comparisons:

a. After comparatives followed by *than* the words *any* and *all* should be followed by *other*.

b. After superlatives followed by *of, any* and *other* should not be used.

4. Avoid mixed comparisons. *John is as good, if not better than she*. If the clause, *if not better*, were left out, this sentence would read, *John is as good than she*. It could be corrected to read, *John is as good **as**, if not better than she*. Similarly, it is wrong to say, *He is one of the greatest, if not the greatest, man in history*.

EXERCISE 22

Choose the correct word from those italicized:

1. The *older oldest* of the three boys was sick.

2. Of Smith and Jones, Smith is the *wealthiest wealthier*.

3. Of two burdens choose the *less least*.

4. Which can run the *fastest faster*, John or Henry?

5. Of the two men, Smith and Jones, the *first former* is the *better best* known.

6. Which is the *larger largest* of the two?

7. Which is the *best better* of the six?

8. Which is the *larger largest* number, six or seven

9. Which is the *more most* desirable, health or wealth?

10. My mother is the *oldest older* of four sisters.

11. The *prettier prettiest* of the twins is the *brighter brightest*.

12. This is the *duller dullest* season of the year.

13. The other is the *worse worst* behaved of the two.

14. Which was the *hotter hottest*, yesterday or to-day?

15. That is the *cleaner cleanest* of the three streets.

EXERCISE 23

Correct any of the following sentences that may be wrong. Give a valid reason for each correction:

1. He was the most active of all his friends.

2. He is the brightest of all his brothers.

3. Of all the other American Colleges, this is the largest.

4. Philadelphia is larger than any city in Pennsylvania.

5. Philadelphia is the largest of all other cities in Pennsylvania.

6. No city in Pennsylvania is so large as Philadelphia.

7. That theory is more universally adopted.

8. He was, of all others, the most clever.

9. This apple is more perfect than that.

10. No fruit is so good as the orange.

11. The orange is better than any fruit.
12. Of all other fruits the orange is the best.
13. The orange is the best of all the fruits.
14. The orange is better than any other fruit.
15. That is the most principal thing in the lesson.
16. Which has been of most importance, steam or electricity?
17. He was more active than any other of his companions.
18. This apple is rounder than that.
19. This apple is more nearly round than that.
20. Paris is the most famous of any other European city.
21. Pennsylvania is the wealthiest of her sister states.
22. No state is so wealthy as Pennsylvania.
23. Pennsylvania is the wealthiest of any of the States.
24. Pennsylvania is wealthier than any of her other sister states.
25. New York is one of the largest, if not the largest city in the world.
26. That book is as good if not better than mine.
27. John is taller than any other boy in his classes.
28. John is taller than any boy in his class.
29. Iron is the most useful of all other metals.
30. Iron is the more useful of the metals.
31. Iron is the most useful of the metals.
32. Of iron and lead, lead is the heaviest.
33. Iron is among the most useful, if not the most useful metal.
34. He is among the oldest if not the oldest of the men in the Senate.
35. That picture is more beautiful than all the pictures.

42. Singular and Plural Adjectives. Some adjectives can be used only with singular nouns and some only with plural nouns. Such adjectives as *one, each, every*, etc., can be used only with singular nouns. Such adjectives as *several, various, many, sundry, two*, etc., can be used only with plural nouns. In many cases, the noun which the adjective modifies is omitted, and the adjective thus acquires the force of a pronoun; as, **Few** *are seen,* **Several** *have come.*

The adjective pronouns *this* and *that* have plural forms, *these* and *those*. The plurals must be used with plural nouns. To say *those kind* is then incorrect. It should be *those kinds*. *Those sort of men* should be *that sort of men* or *those sorts of men*.

43. Either and neither are used to designate one of two objects only. If more than two are referred to, use *any, none, any one, no one*. Note the following correct sentences:

Neither *John nor Henry may go.*

Any one *of the three boys may go.*

44. Each other should be used when referring to two; **one another** when referring to more than two. Note the following correct sentences:

The two brothers love **each other**.

The four brothers love **one another**.

Exercise 24

Correct such of the following sentences as are incorrect. Be able to give reasons:

1. He is six foot tall.
2. I like those kind of fruit.
3. He lost several pound.
4. I have not seen him this twenty year.
5. Have you heard these news?
6. Are they those kind of people?
7. He rode ten mile.
8. There were fifteen car-load of people.
9. These kind of books are interesting.
10. Several phenomenon marked his character.
11. There are a few crisis in every man's career.
12. Each strata of the rock lies at an angle.

13. The poem has six verse in it.

14. Either of the five will do.

15. Little children should love each other.

16. Neither of the large cities in the United States is so large as London.

17. You will be able to find it in either one of those three books.

18. Those two brothers treat one another very coldly.

19. Neither of the many newspapers published an account of it.

20. Either law or medicine is his profession.

21. Some ten box of shoes were on the train.

22. Those two statements contradict one another.

23. The Sahara Desert has several oasis.

24. How can he associate with those sort of men?

45. Placing of Adverbs and Adjectives. In the placing of adjective elements and adverbial elements in the sentence, one should so arrange them as to leave no doubt as to what they are intended to modify.

Wrong: A man was riding on a *horse wearing gray trousers*.

Right: A *man wearing gray trousers* was riding on a horse.

The adverb *only* requires especial attention. Generally *only* should come before the word it is intended to modify. Compare the following correct sentences, and note the differences in meaning.

Only he found the book.

He *only* found the book.

He found *only* the book.

He found the book *only*.

The placing of the words, *almost, ever, hardly, scarcely, merely,* and *quite,* also requires care and thought.

EXERCISE 25

Correct the errors in the location of adjectives and adverbs in the following sentences:

1. I only paid five dollars.
2. I have only done six problems.
3. The clothing business is only profitable in large towns.
4. The school is only open in the evening.
5. I only need ten minutes in which to do it.
6. He had almost climbed to the top when the ladder broke.
7. I never expect to see the like again.
8. A black base-ball player's suit was found.
9. Do you ever remember to have seen the man before?
10. The building was trimmed with granite carved corners.
11. People ceased to wonder gradually.
12. The captain only escaped by hiding in a ditch.
13. I never wish to think of it again.
14. On the trip in that direction he almost went to Philadelphia.
15. Acetylene lamps are only used now in the country.
16. He only spoke of history, not of art.
17. I know hardly what to say.
18. I was merely talking of grammar, not of English literature.
19. The girls were nearly dressed in the same color.
20. He merely wanted to see you.

46. Double Negatives. *I am here* is called an affirmative statement. A denial of that, *I am not here*, is called a negative statement. The words, *not, neither, never, none, nothing*, etc., are all negative words; that is, they serve to make denials of statements.

Two negatives should never be used in the same sentence, since the effect is then to deny the negative you wish to assert, and an affirmative is made where a negative is intended. *We haven't no books*, means that we have some books. The proper negative form would be, *We have no books*, or *We haven't any books*. The mistake occurs usually where such forms as *isn't, don't, haven't*, etc., are used. Examine the following sentences:

Wrong: *It isn't no* use.

Wrong: There *don't none* of them believe it.

Wrong: We *didn't* do *nothing*.

Hardly, scarcely, only, and *but* (in the sense of *only*) are often incorrectly used with a negative. Compare the following right and wrong forms:

Wrong: It was so dark that we *couldn't hardly* see.

Right: It was so dark that we *could hardly* see.

Wrong: There *wasn't only* one person present.

Right: There *was only* one person present.

EXERCISE 26

Correct the following sentences:

1. I can't find it nowhere.
2. For a time I couldn't scarcely tell where I was.
3. They are not allowed to go only on holidays.
4. There isn't but one person that can make the speech.
5. They didn't find no treasure.
6. It won't take but a few minutes to read it all.
7. I haven't seen but two men there.
8. There isn't no one here who knows it.
9. I didn't see no fire; my opinion is that there wasn't no fire.
10. I can't hardly prove that statement.
11. I didn't feel hardly able to go.
12. She couldn't stay only a week.
13. I hadn't scarcely reached shelter when the storm began.
14. You wouldn't scarcely believe that it could be done.
15. He said that he wouldn't bring only his wife.
16. There isn't nothing in the story.
17. He doesn't do nothing.
18. I can't think of nothing but that.

19. He can't hardly mean that.
20. He isn't nowhere near so bright as I.
21. He can't hardly come to-night.
22. It is better to not think nothing about it.
23. She can't only do that.
24. There isn't no use of his objecting to it.
25. There shan't none of them go along with us.
26. Don't never do that again.
27. We could not find but three specimens of the plant.
28. He wasn't scarcely able to walk.
29. He hasn't none of his work prepared.

47. The Articles. *A, an,* and *the*, are called Articles. *A* and *an* are called the **Indefinite Articles**, because they are used to limit the noun to any one thing of a class; as, *a book, a chair.* But *a* or *an* is not used to denote the whole of that class; as, *Silence is golden*, or, *He was elected to the office of President*.

The is called the **Definite Article** because it picks out some one definite individual from a class.

In the sentence, *On the street are **a** brick and **a** stone house*, the article is repeated before each adjective; the effect of this repetition is to make the sentence mean two houses. But, in the sentence, *On the street is **a** brick and stone house*, since the article is used only before the first of the two adjectives, the sentence means that there is only one house and that it is constructed of brick and stone.

Where two nouns refer to the same object, the article need appear only before the first of the two; as, *God, the author and creator of the universe*. But where the nouns refer to two different objects, regarded as distinct from each other, the article should appear before each; as, *He bought a horse and a cow*.

A is used before all words except those beginning with a vowel sound. Before those beginning with a vowel sound *an* is used. If, in a succession of words, one of these forms could not be used before all of the words, then the article must be repeated before each. Thus, one should say, ***An** ax, **a** saw, and **an** adze* (not *An ax, saw and adze*), *made up his outfit*. Generally it is better to repeat the article in each case, whether or not it be the same.

Do not say, *kind of **a house***. Since *a house* is singular, it can have but one kind. Say instead, a *kind of house, a sort of man*, etc.

EXERCISE 27

Correct the following where you think correction is needed:

1. Where did you get that kind of a notion?
2. She is an eager and an ambitious girl.
3. He received the degree of a Master of Arts.
4. The boy and girl came yesterday.
5. Neither the man nor woman was here.
6. He was accompanied by a large and small man.
7. He planted an oak, maple and ash.
8. The third of the team were hurt.
9. The noun and verb will be discussed later.
10. I read a Pittsburg and Philadelphia paper.
11. Read the third and sixth sentence.
12. Read the comments in a monthly and weekly periodical.
13. He is dying from the typhoid fever.
14. He was elected the secretary and the treasurer of the association.
15. What sort of a student are you?
16. He is a funny kind of a fellow.
17. Bring me a new and old chair.
18. That is a sort of a peculiar idea.
19. He was operated upon for the appendicitis.
20. Lock the cat and dog up.

48. No adverb necessary to the sense should be omitted from the sentence. Such improper omission is frequently made when *very* or *too* are used with past participles that are not also recognized as adjectives; as,

Poor: I am *very insulted.* He was *too wrapped* in thought to notice the mistake.

Right: I am *very much insulted.* He was *too much wrapped* in thought to notice the mistake.

EXERCISE 28

Write sentences containing the following adjectives and adverbs. Be sure that they are used correctly.

Both, each, every, only, evidently, hard, latest, awful, terribly, charming, charmingly, lovely, brave, perfect, straight, extreme, very, either, neither, larger, oldest, one, none, hardly, scarcely, only, but, finally, almost, ever, never, new, newly, very.

CHAPTER V

VERBS

49. A **Verb** has already been defined as a word stating something about the subject. Verbs are inflected or changed to indicate the time of the action as past, present, or future; as, *I talk, I talked, I shall talk*, etc. Verbs also vary to indicate completed or incompleted action; as, *I have talked, I shall have talked*, etc. To these variations, which indicate the time of the action, the name **Tense** is given.

The full verbal statement may consist of several words; as, *He **may have gone** home*. Here the verb is *may have gone*. The last word of such a verb phrase is called the **Principal Verb**, and the other words the **Auxiliaries**. In the sentence above, *go (gone)* is the principal verb, and *may* and *have* are the auxiliaries.

50. In constructing the full form of the verb or verb phrase there are three distinct parts from which all other forms are made. These are called the **Principal Parts**.

The First Principal Part, since it is the part by which the verb is referred to as a word, may be called the **Name-Form**. The following are name-forms: *do, see, come, walk, pass*.

The Second Principal Part is called the **Past Tense**. It is formed by adding *ed* to the name-form; as, *walked, pushed, passed*. These verbs that add *ed* are called Regular Verbs. The verb form is often entirely changed; as, *done (do), saw (see), came (come)*. These verbs are called Irregular Verbs.

The Third Principal Part is called the **Past Participle**. It is used mainly in expressing completed action or in the passive voice. In regular verbs the past participle is the same in form as the past tense. In irregular verbs it may differ entirely from both the name-form and the past tense, or it may resemble one or both of them. Examples: *done (do, did), seen (see, saw), come (come, came), set (set, set)*.

51. The name-form, when unaccompanied by auxiliaries, is used with all subjects, except those in the third person singular, to assert action in the present time or present tense; as, *I go, We come, You see, Horses run*.

The name-form is also used with various auxiliaries (*may, might, can, must, will, should, shall*, etc.) to assert futurity, determination, possibility, possession, etc. Examples: *I may go, We shall come, You can see, Horses should run*.

By preceding it with the word *to*, the name-form is used to form what is called the **Present Infinitive**; as, *I wish to go, I hope to see.*

What may be called the **s-form** of the verb, or the **singular** form, is usually constructed by adding *s* or *es* to the name-form. The s-form is used with singular subjects in the third person; as, *He goes, She comes, It runs, The dog trots.*

The s-form is found in the third personal singular of the present tense. In other tenses, if present at all, the s-form is in the auxiliary, where the present tense of the auxiliary is used to form some other tense of the principal verb. Examples: *He has* (present tense), *He has gone* (perfect tense), *He has been seen.*

Some verbs have no s-form; as, *will, shall, may*. The verb *be* has two irregular s-forms: *Is*, in the present tense, and *was* in the past tense. The s-form of *have* is *has*.

52. The past tense always stands alone in the predicate; i. e., **it should never be used with any auxiliaries**. To use it so, however, is one of the most frequent errors in grammar. The following are past tense forms: *went, saw, wore, tore*. To say, therefore, *I have saw, I have went, It was tore, They were wore*, would be grossly incorrect.

53. The third principal part, the past participle, on the other hand, **can never be used as a predicate verb without an auxiliary**. The following are distinctly past participle forms: *done, seen, sung*, etc. One could not then properly say, *I seen, I done, I sung*, etc.

The distinction as to use with and without auxiliaries applies, of course, only to irregular verbs. In regular verbs, the past tense and past participle are always the same, and so no error could result from their confusion.

The past participle is used to form the *Perfect Infinitives*; as, *to have gone, to have seen, to have been seen.*

54. The following is a list of the principal parts of the most important irregular verbs. The list should be mastered thoroughly. The student should bear in mind always that, **the past tense form should never be used with an auxiliary**, and that **the past participle form should never be used as a predicate verb without an auxiliary**.

In some instances verbs have been included in the list below which are always regular in their forms, or which have both regular and irregular forms. These are verbs for whose principal parts incorrect forms are often used.

PRINCIPAL PARTS OF VERBS

Name-form	Past Tense	Past Participle
awake	awoke or awaked	awaked
begin	began	begun
beseech	besought	besought
bid (to order or to greet)	bade	bidden or bid
bid (at auction)	bid	bidden or bid
blow	blew	blown
break	broke	broken
burst	burst	burst
choose	chose	chosen
chide	chid	chidden or chid
come	came	come
deal	dealt	dealt
dive	dived	dived

Name-form	Past Tense	Past Participle
do	did	done
draw	drew	drawn
drink	drank	drunk or drank
drive	drove	driven
eat	ate	eaten
fall	fell	fallen
flee	fled	fled
fly	flew	flown
forsake	forsook	forsaken
forget	forgot	forgot or forgotten

freeze	froze	frozen
get	got	got (gotten)
give	gave	given
go	went	gone
hang (clothes)	hung	hung
hang (a man)	hanged	hanged
know	knew	known
lay	laid	laid
lie	lay	lain
mean	meant	meant
plead	pleaded	pleaded
prove	proved	proved
ride	rode	ridden
raise	raised	raised
rise	rose	risen
run	ran	run
see	saw	seen
seek	sought	sought
set	set	set
shake	shook	shaken
shed	shed	shed
shoe	shod	shod
sing	sang	sung
sit	sat	sat
slay	slew	slain

Name-form	Past Tense	Past Participle
sink	sank	sunk
speak	spoke	spoken
steal	stole	stolen
swim	swam	swum
take	took	taken
teach	taught	taught
tear	tore	torn
throw	threw	thrown
tread	trod	trod or trodden
wake	woke or waked	woke or waked
wear	wore	worn
weave	wove	woven
write	wrote	written

NOTES.—*Ought* has no past participle. It may then never be used with an auxiliary. *I had ought to go* is incorrect. The idea would be amply expressed by *I ought to go*.

Model conjugations of the verbs *to be* and *to see* in all forms are given under §77 at the end of this chapter.

EXERCISE 29

In the following sentences change the italicized verb so as to use the past tense, and then so as to use the past participle:

Example: (Original sentence), *The guests begin to go home.*

(Changed to past tense), *The guests began to go home.*

(Changed to past participle), *The guests have begun to go home.*

1. Our books *lie* on the mantel.
2. John *comes* in and *lays* his books on the desk.
3. I *see* the parade.

4. He *runs* up the road.
5. They *set* their chairs in a row.
6. The noise *wakes* me.
7. Cæsar *bids* him enter.
8. If they *prove* their innocence, they should be discharged.
9. His friends *plead* strongly for him.
10. Do you know what they *mean* by that?
11. I *awake* early every morning.
12. He *begins* to think of strange things.
13. The children *beseech* me to go with them.
14. My mother *bids* me to say that she will be here at six.
15. Smith *bids* fifty dollars for the chair.
16. My servants *break* many dishes.
17. They *choose* their associates.
18. The box *bursts* open.
19. His mother *chides* him for his misbehavior.
20. He *comes* here every day.
21. I *deal* there this week.
22. The boys *dive* beautifully.
23. You *do* so much more than is necessary.
24. They *draw* lots for the watch.
25. Jones *drinks* this wine very seldom.
26. They *drive* over to Milton once a week.
27. They *drive* a sorrel horse.
28. The cows *eat* grass.
29. The Gauls *flee* before Cæsar.
30. The swallows all *fly* into the chimney at evening.
31. They *forsake* the cause without any reason.
32. Cæsar *gives* them no answer.

33. They *get* no money for their services.
34. You *forget* that we have no right to do that.
35. Water *freezes* at thirty-two degrees Fahrenheit.
36. The ball *goes* to the opposing team.
37. You *hang* the rope on the tree.
38. The sheriff *hangs* the murderer at noon.
39. I *know* of nothing more worrying.
40. She *lays* the knife on the table.
41. They *lie* in bed until eleven.
42. Why they *rise* so late, I do not know.
43. They *raise* no objection.
44. John *runs* very rapidly.
45. You *sit* very quietly.
46. Cæsar *seeks* to learn the intention of the enemy.
47. The politician vigorously *shakes* all hands.
48. The roof *sheds* water in all storms.
49. The blacksmith *shoes* horses.
50. The choir *sings* for each service.
51. You *speak* too rapidly to be easily understood.
52. Few men *steal* because they want to.
53. I *swim* one hundred yards very readily.
54. They *teach* all the elementary branches there.
55. You *take* all subscriptions for the concert.
56. Those clothes *tear* readily.
57. They *tread* the grapes in making wine.
58. Who *throws* paper on the floor?
59. I always *wear* old clothes in which to work.
60. She *writes* to her mother daily.
61. They *weave* the best rugs in Philadelphia.

EXERCISE 30

Write original sentences containing the following verbs, correctly used:

Begun, blew, bidden, bad, chose, broke, come, dealt, dived, drew, driven, flew, forsook, froze, given, give, gave, went, hanged, knew, rode, pleaded, ran, seen, saw, shook, shod, sung, slew, spoke, swum, taken, torn, wore, threw, woven, wrote, written.

EXERCISE 31

Insert the proper form of the verb in the following sentences. The verb to be used is in black-faced type at the beginning of each group:

1. **Begin.** He —— to act at once. The reports —— to disturb him a little. He has —— to feel hurt over them.

2. **Bid.** The proprietor —— us a pleasant good day. No matter how much he —— the auctioneer will not hear him. We were —— to enter.

3. **Blow.** The cornetist —— with all his might. The ship was —— about all day. The wind does —— terrifically sometimes. It may —— to-night. The wind —— all last night.

4. **Break.** He fell and —— his leg. It is well that his neck was not ——.

5. **Burst.** During the battle the shells frequently —— right over us. Oaken casks have often ——.

6. **Chide.** He —— us frequently about our actions. He was never —— himself.

7. **Choose.** They —— him president. They have —— wisely.

8. **Come.** He —— at nine to-day. He has always —— earlier heretofore. Let him —— when he wishes.

9. **Deal.** Before explaining the game, he —— out the cards.

10. **Dive.** Twice last summer he —— off the bridge.

11. **Do.** Thou canst not say I —— it. He often —— it.

12. **Draw.** The picture was —— by a famous artist. He formerly —— very well, but I think that now he —— very poorly.

13. **Drive.** The horse was —— twenty miles. He almost —— it to death.

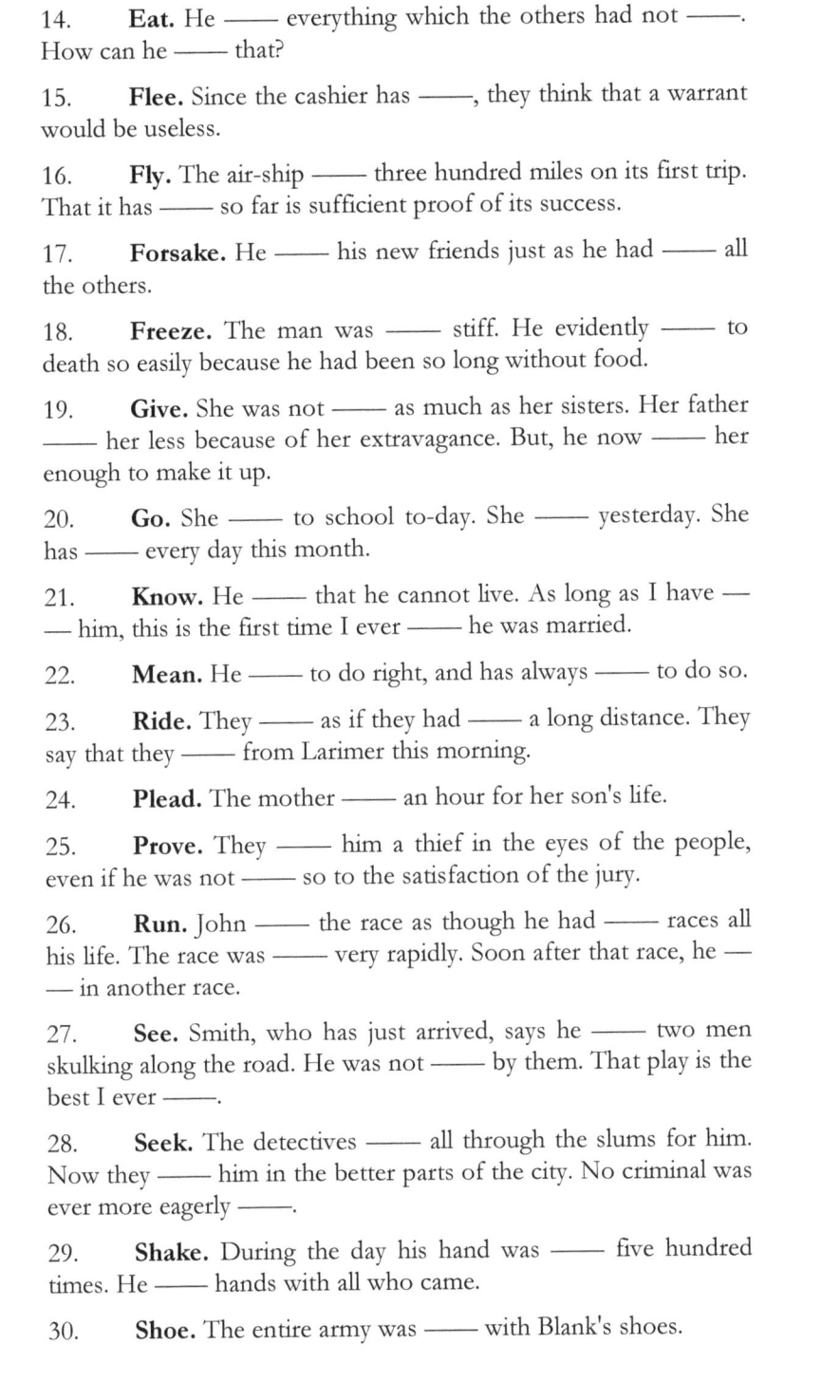

14. **Eat.** He —— everything which the others had not ——. How can he —— that?

15. **Flee.** Since the cashier has ——, they think that a warrant would be useless.

16. **Fly.** The air-ship —— three hundred miles on its first trip. That it has —— so far is sufficient proof of its success.

17. **Forsake.** He —— his new friends just as he had —— all the others.

18. **Freeze.** The man was —— stiff. He evidently —— to death so easily because he had been so long without food.

19. **Give.** She was not —— as much as her sisters. Her father —— her less because of her extravagance. But, he now —— her enough to make it up.

20. **Go.** She —— to school to-day. She —— yesterday. She has —— every day this month.

21. **Know.** He —— that he cannot live. As long as I have —— him, this is the first time I ever —— he was married.

22. **Mean.** He —— to do right, and has always —— to do so.

23. **Ride.** They —— as if they had —— a long distance. They say that they —— from Larimer this morning.

24. **Plead.** The mother —— an hour for her son's life.

25. **Prove.** They —— him a thief in the eyes of the people, even if he was not —— so to the satisfaction of the jury.

26. **Run.** John —— the race as though he had —— races all his life. The race was —— very rapidly. Soon after that race, he —— in another race.

27. **See.** Smith, who has just arrived, says he —— two men skulking along the road. He was not —— by them. That play is the best I ever ——.

28. **Seek.** The detectives —— all through the slums for him. Now they —— him in the better parts of the city. No criminal was ever more eagerly ——.

29. **Shake.** During the day his hand was —— five hundred times. He —— hands with all who came.

30. **Shoe.** The entire army was —— with Blank's shoes.

31. **Sing.** The choir —— the anthem as they had never —— it before. They always —— it well.

32. **Sink.** The stone —— as soon as it is in the water. The ship was —— in forty fathoms of water. They —— the ship in 1861.

33. **Speak.** Though they claimed that they always —— to her, she was really never —— to by any member of the family.

34. **Steal.** The money was ——; whether or not he —— it I do not know. Everyone believes that he has frequently —— goods from the store.

35. **Take.** I was —— for him several times that day. No one ever —— me for him before.

36. **Teach.** John —— school every day. He has —— for ten years. He first —— when he was eighteen years old.

37. **Tear.** The dog —— at the paper until it was —— entirely to pieces. He —— up everything he finds.

38. **Throw.** He was —— by a horse which never before —— anyone.

39. **Wear.** The trousers were —— entirely out in a month, but I —— the coat and vest for six months.

40. **Weave.** This carpet was —— at Philadelphia. The manufacturers say they never —— a better one, and they —— the best in the country.

41. **Write.** Although he has —— several times, he has never —— anything about that. He —— to me just last week. He —— at least once a month.

EXERCISE 32

Correct the errors in the use of verbs in the following sentences:

1. He plead all day to be released.
2. The horse was rode to death.
3. The letter was wrote before he knowed the truth.
4. He was immediately threw out of the room.
5. She run around all day and then was sick the next day.
6. I never seen anything like it.

7. He was very much shook by the news.
8. The matter was took up by the committee.
9. The horse has been stole from the owner.
10. Goliath was slew by David.
11. The words have been spoke in anger.
12. I have went to church every day.
13. Was the river froze enough for skating?
14. He begun to take notice immediately.
15. The umbrella was blew to pieces.
16. I have broke my ruler.
17. Jones was chose as leader of the class.
18. He said he come as soon as he could.
19. I done it.
20. I have never did anything so foolish.
21. I have ate all that was in the lunch-box.
22. The horse was drove ten miles.

EXERCISE 33

Write sentences in which the following verb forms are properly used:

begun, blew, broke, chose, come, came, done, did, drew, drunk, drove, ate, flew, forsook, froze, forgot, gave, give, went, hang, hung, knew, rode, run, shook, sung, slew, spoke, stole, took, tore, threw, wore, wrote.

55. Transitive and Intransitive Verbs. A **Transitive Verb** is one in which the action of the verb goes over to a receiver; as, *He **killed** the horse, I **keep** my word.* In both these sentences, the verb serves to transfer the action from the subject to the object or receiver of the action. The verbs in these sentences, and all similar verbs, are transitive verbs. All others, in which the action does not go to a receiver, are called **Intransitive Verbs**.

56. Active and Passive Voice. The **Active Voice** represents the subject as the doer of the action; as, *I tell, I see, He makes chairs.* The **Passive Voice** represents the subject as the receiver of the action; as, *I am told, I am seen, I have been seen, Chairs are made by me.* Since only transitive verbs can have a receiver of the action, only transitive verbs can have both active and passive voice.

57. There are a few special verbs in which the failure to distinguish between the transitive and the intransitive verbs leads to frequent error. The most important of these verbs are the following: *sit, set, awake, wake, lie, lay, rise, arise, raise, fell,* and *fall*. Note again the principal parts of these verbs:

wake (to rouse another)	woke, waked	woke, waked
awake (to cease to sleep)	awoke, awaked	awaked
fell (to strike down)	felled	felled
fall (to topple over)	fell	fallen
lay (to place)	laid	laid
lie (to recline)	lay	lain
raise (to cause to ascend)	raised	raised
(a)rise (to ascend)	(a)rose	(a)risen
set (to place)	set	set
sit (to rest)	sat	sat

The first of each pair of the above verbs is transitive, and the second is intransitive. Only the first, then, of each pair can have an object or can be used in the passive voice.

NOTES.—The following exceptions in the use of *sit* and *set* are, by reason of usage, regarded as correct: *The sun sets, The moon sets, They sat themselves down to rest,* and *He set out for Chicago.*

Lie, meaning to deceive, has for its principal parts, *lie, lied, lied. Lie*, however, with this meaning is seldom confused with *lie* meaning to recline. The present participle of *lie* is *lying*.

Compare the following sentences, and note the reasons why the second form in each case is the correct form.

WRONG   RIGHT

Awake me early to-morrow.	Wake me early to-morrow.
He was awoke by the noise.	He was woke (waked) by the noise.
He has fallen a tree.	He has felled a tree.
I have laid down.	I have lain down.
I lay the book down (past tense).	I laid the book down.
The river has raised.	The river has risen.
He raised in bed.	He rose in bed.
I set there.	I sat there.
I sat the chair there.	I set the chair there.

EXERCISE 34

Form an original sentence showing the proper use of each of the following words:

Lie, lay (to place), sit, set, sat, sitting, setting, lie (to recline), lie (to deceive), lying, laying, rise, arose, raised, raise, fell (to topple over), fallen, felled, awake, wake, awaked, woke, falling, felling, rising, raising, waking, awaking, lain, laid, lied.

EXERCISE 35

Correct such of the following sentences as are wrong:

1. Let sleeping dogs lay.
2. The sun has sat in the golden west.
3. He has laid in bed all morning.
4. He will sit out on his journey this morning.
5. Let him sit there as long as he wishes.
6. He sat the chair by the table.
7. He awoke everybody at daylight.
8. He laid down to sleep.
9. Let him lie there until he wakes.
10. The shower has lain the dust.
11. The curtain raised because it was raised by his orders.
12. The river has risen four feet.

13. Falling trees is his amusement.
14. To have been awaked then would have been sad.
15. To have waked then would have been sad.
16. Waking at dawn, they renewed the journey.
17. He has set there all day.
18. He lay the papers before the judge.
19. The judge laid the papers aside.
20. Lieing in the shade is his most strenuous occupation.

EXERCISE 36

In the following sentences fill the blanks with the proper forms of the verbs indicated:

SIT AND SET

1. I —— in that seat all the evening.
2. Please —— here until I return.
3. He was still ——ting there on my return.
4. The sun —— in the west.
5. He —— out for home yesterday.
6. —— down and rest awhile.
7. James —— down and talked to me.
8. He was engaged in ——ting out flowers.
9. I —— the bucket on the rock above the bridge.
10. Last evening we —— at the table for more than an hour.
11. —— here until I call my mother.
12. —— the lamp on the table.
13. He has —— there all day.
14. The chair was —— by the desk.
15. I usually —— up until twelve.
16. She —— the hen on some eggs and she remained —— there.
17. She told me to —— there, and I —— down.
18. By whom has the lamp been —— there?

19. I —— my chair by the window and —— there all the afternoon.

20. How can she —— still for so long?

21. The moon —— at twelve.

LAY AND LIE

1. I —— down this afternoon to rest.

2. I —— in bed until late every morning.

3. I have frequently —— in bed until eleven.

4. He always —— his books on the desk.

5. He just now —— his books on the desk.

6. He has —— them there every morning.

7. His books have sometimes —— there all day.

8. His books have sometimes been ——ing there before I arrive.

9. 9. After he —— down he remembered that he had left a letter on his desk.

10. Will it not be well for you to —— down for a while?

11. I —— on the grass yesterday for an hour or more.

12. I have —— down and feel much better.

13. Now I —— me down to sleep.

14. The scene of the play is —— in rural Pennsylvania.

15. The tramps —— behind the barn waiting for dawn.

16. I had —— down to rest before (set or sit) ting out on my journey.

17. The floor was —— by an expert carpenter.

18. She told me to —— the matter before the teacher.

19. —— down, Fido.

20. When we are weary, we —— down.

21. Who —— that on the table?

22. He has repeatedly —— about the matter.

23. He —— without the slightest hesitation.

24.   ———ing down is a good way to rest.

25.   ———ing is a sin.

26.   He ——— to his father, and his father knew it.

RAISE AND RISE (ARISE)

1.   I will ——— and go unto my father.

2.   He has ——— early to-day.

3.   I do not know why he ——— so early.

4.   ——— your hand if you know.

5.   Everyone ——— his hand.

6.   They have all ——— their hands.

7.   All their hands were ——— at once.

8.   The price of meat has ———.

9.   The bread would not ———.

10.   I ——— in order that I might see better.

11.   The flag was very carefully ———.

12.   He tried to ——— himself from the condition into which he had fallen.

13.   The curtain is to ——— at eight. I myself shall see to ———ing it then.

14.   The boy ——— and answers.

15.   He is ——— rapidly to prominence.

16.   Will you please ——— the window?

17.   The safe was ——— by means of a rope.

18.   It is like trying to ——— one's self by one's boot-straps.

19.   ——— and march to the front of the room.

20.   The river ——— rapidly.

FELL AND FALL

1.   Gladstone, when living, ——— a tree each morning for exercise.

2.   To ——— an ox with one blow of the fist is a feat of wonderful strength.

3. He was —— to the earth by a blow from a club.

4. To —— often is to be expected in learning to skate.

5. ——ing down is a small matter to the young.

6. He has often —— from the roof of the porch.

7. After he —— once, he seemed to try to do so again.

8. I did not see him——.

9. Not a shot is fired but a bird ——.

10. Let the tree be —— across the road.

11. It is hard to avoid ——ing on the ice.

AWAKE AND WAKE

1. Have them —— me very early.

2. He went upstairs and —— his brother.

3. His brother did not wish to be —— so early.

4. This morning I —— at dawn.

5. It is unpleasant to —— so early.

6. You say that you have never —— after nine?

7. Who —— so early, this morning?

8. He would not say who —— him.

9. ——ing in the dead of night is unpleasant.

10. ——ing everybody up by their noise is an every night occurrence.

11. The sun —— me early.

12. The whole country-side seemed to —— at once.

13. He had himself —— at six o'clock.

58. Mode. Mode is that form of the verb which indicates the manner in which the action or state is to be regarded. There are several modes in English, but only between the indicative and subjunctive modes is the distinction important. Generally speaking, the **Indicative Mode** is used when the statement is regarded as a fact or as truth, and the **Subjunctive Mode** is used when the statement expresses uncertainty or implies some degree of doubt.

59. Forms of the Subjunctive. The places in which the subjunctive differs from the indicative are in the present and past tenses of the verb *be*, and in the present tense of active verbs. The following outline will show the difference between the indicative and the subjunctive of *be*:

INDICATIVE PRESENT OF BE		INDICATIVE PAST OF BE	
I am	we are	I was	we were
thou art	you are	thou wert or wast	you were
he (she, it) is	they are	he (she, it) was	they were

SUBJUNCTIVE PRESENT OF BE		SUBJUNCTIVE PAST OF BE	
If I be	If we be	If I were	If we were
If thou be	If you be	If thou were	If you were
If he (she, it) be	If they be	If he (she, it) were	If they were

If is used only as an example of the conjunctions on which the subjunctive depends. Other conjunctions may be used, or the verb may precede the subject.

NOTE.—It will be noticed that *thou art* and *thou wast*, etc., have been used in the second person singular. Strictly speaking, these are the proper forms to be used here, even though *you are* and *you were*, etc., are customarily used in addressing a single person.

In the subjunctive of *be*, it will be noted that the form *be* is used throughout the present tense; and the form *were* throughout the past tense.

In other verbs the subjunctive, instead of having the s-form in the third person singular of the present tense, has the name-form, or the same form as all the other forms of the present tense; as, indicative, *he runs, she sees, it seems, he has;* subjunctive, *if he run, though she see, lest it seem, if he have.*

NOTE.—An examination of the model conjugations under §77 will give a further understanding of the forms of the subjunctive.

60. Use of Indicative and Subjunctive. The indicative mode would be properly used in the following sentence, when the statement is regarded as true: *If that evidence is true, then he is a criminal.* Similarly: *If he is rich, he ought to be charitable.* Most directly declarative statements are put in the indicative mode.

But when the sense of the statement shows uncertainty in the speaker's mind, or shows that the condition stated is regarded as contrary to fact or as untrue, the subjunctive is used. Note the two sentences following, in which the conditions are properly in the subjunctive: *If those statements be true, then all statements are true, Were I rich, I might be charitable.*

The subjunctive is usually preceded by the conjunctions, *if, though, lest, although,* or the verb precedes the subject. But it must be borne in mind that these do not always indicate the subjunctive mode. **The use of the subjunctive depends on whether the condition is regarded as a fact or as contrary to fact, certain or uncertain.**

It should be added that the subjunctive is perhaps going out of use; some of the best writers no longer use its forms. This passing of the subjunctive is to be regretted and to be discouraged, since its forms give opportunity for many fine shades of meaning.

EXERCISE 37

*Write five sentences which illustrate the correct use of **be** in the third person singular without an auxiliary, and five which illustrate the correct use of **were** in the third person singular.*

EXERCISE 38

Choose the preferable form in the following sentences, and be able to give a definite reason for your choice. In some of the sentences either form may be used correctly:

1. He acts as if it *were was* possible always to escape death.
2. If it *was were* near enough, I should walk.
3. If I *was were* only wealthy!
4. If I *were was* in his place, I should study medicine.
5. If you *are be* right, then the book is wrong.
6. If he *was were* I, he would come.
7. Though he *was were* very economical, he remained poor.
8. Though she *was were* an angel, I should dislike her.
9. If he *be is* there, ask him to pay the bill.
10. If he *be is* there, he makes no sign of his presence.

11. If this *be is* wrong, then all love of country is wrong.

12. If it *rains rain*, I stay at school.

13. Take care lest you *are be* deceived by appearances.

14. Would that I *was were* a bird.

15. If it *snow snows*, I can't come.

16. If your father *comes come*, bring him to dinner.

17. If your father *was were* here, you would act differently.

18. Though he *were was* king over all the earth I should despise him.

19. If he *come comes*, he will find me at home.

20. *Was were* it necessary, I should jump.

21. If to-morrow *be is* pleasant, we shall go driving.

22. If my mother *was were* here, she would say I might go.

23. If she *was were* at home, I did not hear of it.

24. If that *is be* his motive, he is unworthy.

25. Though this *seem seems* improbable, it is true.

26. If a speech *is be* praised by none but literary men, it is bad.

27. If the father *pays pay* the debt, he will be released.

28. Though Mary *be is* young, she is a writer of note.

29. Unless he *takes take* better care of his health, he will die.

30. If he *be is* honest, he has not shown it.

31. If he *be is* honest, he will insist on paying me.

32. If he ever *tell tells* the truth, he conceals the fact.

61. Agreement of Verb with its Subject. The verb should agree with its subject in person and number. The most frequent error is the failure of the verb to agree in number with its subject. Singular subjects are used with plural verbs, and plural subjects with singular verbs. These errors arise chiefly from a misapprehension of the true number of the subject.

The s-form of the verb is the only distinct singular form, and occurs only in the third person, singular, present indicative; as, *He runs, she goes, it moves*. *Is, was*, and *has* are the singular forms of the auxiliaries. *Am* is used only with a subject in the first person, and is not a source of confusion. The other auxiliaries have no singular forms.

Failure of the verb and its subject to agree in person seldom occurs, and so can cause little confusion.

Examine the following correct forms of agreement of verb and subject:

A barrel of clothes **was** shipped (not *were shipped*).

A man and a woman **have** been here (not *has been here*).

Boxes **are** scarce (not *is scarce*).

When **were** the brothers here (not *when was*)?

62. Agreement of Subject and Verb in Number. The general rule to be borne in mind in regard to number, is that **it is the meaning and not the form of the subject that determines whether to use the singular or the plural form of the verb.** This rule also applies to the use of singular or plural pronouns.

Many nouns plural in form are singular in meaning; as, *politics, measles, news,* etc.

Many, also, are treated as plurals, though in meaning they are singular; as, *forceps, tongs, trousers.*

Some nouns, singular in form, are, according to the sense in which, they are used, either singular or plural in meaning; as, *committee, family, pair, jury, assembly, means.* The following sentences are all correct: *The assembly has closed its meeting, The assembly are all total abstainers, The whole family is a famous one, The whole family are sick.*

In the use of the adjective pronouns, *some, each*, etc., the noun is often omitted. When this is done, error is often made by using the wrong number of the verb. *Each, either, neither, this, that*, and *one*, when used alone as subjects, require singular verbs. *All, those, these, few, many*, always require plural verbs. *Any, none,* and *some* may take either singular or plural verbs. In most of these cases, as is true throughout the subject of agreement in number, reason will determine the form to be used.

Some nouns in a plural form express quantity rather than number. When quantity is plainly intended the singular verb should be used. Examine the following sentences; each is correct: *Three drops of medicine is a dose, Ten thousand tons of coal was purchased by the firm, Two hundred dollars was the amount of the collection, Two hundred silver dollars were in the collection.*

EXERCISE 39

In each of the following sentences, by giving a reason, justify the correctness of the agreement in number of the verb and the noun:

1. The jury have agreed.
2. The jury has been sent out to reconsider its verdict.
3. The committee has presented its report, but they have differed in regard to one matter.
4. The whole tribe was destroyed.
5. The tribe were scattered through the different states.
6. The regiment were almost all sick.
7. A variety of persons was there.
8. The society meets each month.
9. The society is divided in its opinion.
10. A number were unable to be present.
11. A great number was present.
12. The number present was great.
13. What means were used to gain his vote?
14. That means of gaining votes is corrupt.
15. Seventeen pounds was the cat's weight.
16. Twenty years of his life was spent in prison.
17. Two hundred pounds was his weight.
18. The family are all at home.
19. The family is large.
20. A pair of gloves has been lost.
21. A pair of twins were sitting in the doorway.
22. The army was defeated.

EXERCISE 40

Construct sentences in which each of the words named below is used correctly as the subject of some one of the verbs, ***is, was, has, have, are, was, have, go, goes, run, runs, come, comes:***

One, none, nobody, everybody, this, that, these, those, former, latter, few, some, many, other, any, all, such, news, pains, measles, gallows, ashes, dregs, goods, pincers, thanks, victuals, vitals, mumps, flock, crowd, fleet, group, choir, class, army, mob, tribe, herd, committee, tons, dollars, bushels, carloads, gallons, days, months.

EXERCISE 41

Go over each of the above sentences and determine whether **it** *or* **they** *should be used in referring to the subject.*

63. The following rules govern the agreement of the verb with a compound subject:

1. When a singular noun is modified by two adjectives so as to mean two distinct things, the verb should be in the plural; as, *French and German literature* **are** *studied.*

2. When the verb applies to the different parts of the compound subject, the plural form of the verb should be used; as, *John and Harry* **are** *still to come.*

3. When the verb applies to one subject and not to the others, it should agree with that subject to which it applies; as, *The employee, and not the employers,* **was** *to blame, The employers, and not the employee,* **were** *to blame, The boy, as well as his sisters,* **deserves** *praise.*

4. When the verb applies separately to several subjects, each in the singular, the verb should be singular; as, *Each book and each paper* **was** *in its place, No help and no hope* **is** *found for him, Either one or the other* **is** *he, Neither one nor the other* **is** *he.*

5. When the verb applies separately to several subjects, some of which are singular and some plural, it should agree with the subject nearest to it; as, *Neither the boy, nor his sisters* **deserve** *praise, Neither the sisters nor the boy* **deserves** *praise.*

6. When a verb separates its subjects, it should agree with the first; as, *The leader* **was** *slain and all his men, The men* **were** *slain, and also the leader.*

EXERCISE 42

Choose the proper form of the verb in the following sentences:

1. Hard and soft coal *is are* used.
2. The boy and the girl *have has* come.
3. Neither James nor I *are is* to go.

4. Neither James nor they *are is* to go.

5. Henry, and not his sister, *is are* sure to be invited.

6. The children and their father *was were* on the train.

7. Each man and each woman *was were* present.

8. Either Tennyson or Wordsworth *was were* the author of that poem.

9. Either the man or his children *was were* lost.

10. Either the children or their father *was were* lost.

11. Bread and milk *are is* frugal but wholesome fare.

12. The teacher *was were* cut off by the fire, and also her pupils.

13. The pupils *was were* cut off by the fire, and also the teacher.

14. Dogs and cats *is are* useless animals.

15. Neither the daughters nor their mother *is are* at home.

16. Either the soldier or his officers *is are* mistaken.

17. The cat and all her kittens *was were* at the door.

18. Tennyson, not Wordsworth, *were was* the author.

19. Each of the trustees *has have* a vote.

20. Our success or our failure *is are* due solely to ourselves.

21. Neither sincerity nor cordiality *characterize characterizes* him.

22. Everyone of these chairs *is are* mine.

23. Each day and each hour *bring brings* new questions.

24. The car and all its passengers *was were* blown up.

25. The ambition and activity of the man *has have* been the *cause causes* of his success.

26. Old and new hay *is are* equally good for horses.

27. Matthew or Paul *are is* responsible for that belief.

28. A man, a woman, and a child *is are* comprised in the group.

29. The pupils and also the teacher *were was* embarrassed.

30. The teacher and also the pupils *were was* embarrassed.

31. Neither he nor I *are is am* going.

32. Book after book *was were* taken from the shelves.//
33. Either Aunt Mary or her daughters *is are* coming.//
34. Either the daughters or Aunt Mary *is are* coming.//
35. Aunt Mary, but not her daughters, *is are* coming.//
36. The daughters, but not Aunt Mary, *is are* coming.//
37. Both Aunt Mary and her daughter *is are* coming.//
38. Mary, and not her mother, *is are* coming.//
39. No preacher and no woman *is are* allowed to enter.//
40. Every adult man and woman *has have* a vote.//
41. Money, if not culture, *gains gain* a way.//
42. Brain power, as well as money, *talk talks*.//
43. Each boy and girl *bring brings* books.

64. Some miscellaneous cautions in regard to agreement in number:

1. Do not use a plural verb after a singular subject modified by an adjective phrase; as, *The thief, with all his booty, was captured.*

2. Do not use a singular form of the verb after *you* and *they*. Say: *You were, they are, they were*, etc., not, *you was, they was*, etc.

3. Do not mistake a noun modifier for the noun subject. In the sentence, *The **sale** of boxes was increased*, *sale*, not *boxes*, is the subject of the verb.

4. When the subject is a relative pronoun, the number and the person of the antecedent determine the number and the person of the verb. Both of the following sentences are correct: *He is the only one of the men **that is** to be trusted, He is one of those men **that are** to be trusted.* It is to be remembered that the singulars and the plurals of the relative pronouns are alike in form; *that, who*, etc., may refer to one or more than one.

5. Do not use incorrect contractions of the verb with *not*. *Don't* cannot be used with *he* or *she* or *it*, or with any other singular subject in the third person. One should say, *He doesn't*, not *he don't; it doesn't*, not *it don't; man doesn't*, not *man don't*. The proper form of the verb that is being contracted in these instances is *does*, not *do*. *Ain't* and *hain't* are always wrong; no such contractions are recognized. Such colloquial contractions as *don't, can't*, etc., should not be used at all in formal composition.

Exercise 43

Correct such of the following sentences as are wrong:

1. The ship, with all her crew, were lost.

2. You was there, John, was you not?

3. They was never known to do that before.

4. A barrel of apples were sold

5. How many were there who was there?

6. This is one of the books that is always read.

7. He don't know his own relatives.

8. I ain't coming to-night.

9. The art gallery, with all its pictures, was destroyed.

10. John, when was you in the city?

11. The book, with all its errors, is valuable.

12. Who they was, I couldn't tell.

13. This is one of the mountains which are called "The Triplets."

14. This is one of the eleven pictures that has gained prizes.

15. The hands of the clock is wrong.

16. The gallery of pictures are splendid.

17. This is one of those four metals that is valuable.

18. This is the one of those four metals that are valuable.

19. That answer, as you will see, hain't right.

20. The whole box of books were shipped.

EXERCISE 44

In the following sentences correct such as are wrong:

1. "Cows" are a common noun.

2. Such crises seldom occurs.

3. Fifty dollars were given him as a present.

4. There were four men, each of which were sent by a different bank.

5. At that time the morals of men were very low.

6. Mathematics are my most interesting study.

7. There was once two boys who was imprisoned in the Tower.

8. The jury is delivering its verdict.

9. The "Virginians" is a famous book.

10. Ten minutes were given him in which to answer.

11. Everyone of these farms are mine.

12. Lee, with his whole army, surrender.

13. Farm after farm were passed by the train.

14. He is one of the greatest men that has ever been president.

15. Three hundred miles of wires were cut down.

16. Three fourths of his time are wasted.

17. Three quarts of oats is all that is needed.

18. A variety of sounds charms the ear.

19. A variety of recitations were given.

20. The committee have adjourned.

21. Washington was one of the greatest generals that has ever lived.

22. Take one of the books that is lying on the table.

23. The house is one of those that overlooks the bay.

24. Question after question were propounded to him.

25. He was one of the best orators that has been produced by the school.

26. He is one of those persons who are quick to learn.

27. A black and white horse were in the ring.

28. A black and a white horse was in the ring.

29. The committee disagree on some points.

30. Mary, where was you yesterday?

31. The end and aim of his life are to get money.

32. All the crop were lost.

33. One of them are gone.

34. There comes the children.
35. Were either of these men elected?
36. The alumni of this school is not very loyal.
37. There seem to be few here.
38. There seems to be a few here.
39. Neither of the letters were received.
40. In all those songs there are a sprightliness and charm.
41. The Association of Engineers are still flourishing.
42. Neither John nor Henry have come.
43. Either this book or that are wrong.
44. This book and that is wrong.
45. This book, not that, is wrong.
46. Either this book or those students is wrong.
47. Either those students, or this book is wrong.
48. This chemical with its compounds were the agents used in tanning.

65. Use of Shall and Will. The use of the auxiliaries, *shall* and *will*, with their past tenses, is a source of very many errors. The following outline will show the correct use of *shall* and *will*, except in dependent clauses and questions:

To indicate simple futurity or probability:

Use *shall* with *I* and *we*; use *will* with all other subjects.

To indicate promise, determination, threat, or command on the part of the speaker; i. e., action which the speaker means to control;

Use *will* with *I* and *we*; use *shall* with all other subjects.

Examine the following examples of the correct use of *shall* and *will*:

Statements as to probable future events:

We shall probably be there.
I think *you will* want to be there.
It will rain before night.

Statements of determination on the part of the speaker:

I will come in spite of his command.
You shall go home.
It shall not happen again, I promise you.

66. Shall and Will in Questions. In interrogative sentences *shall* should always be used with the first person. In the second and third persons that auxiliary should be used which is logically expected in the answer.

Examine the agreement in the use of *shall* and *will* in the following questions and answers:

QUESTIONS.	ANSWERS.
Shall I miss the car?	You *will* miss it.
Shall you be there?	I think I *shall* (probability).
Will he do it?	I think he *will* (assertion).
Shall your son obey the teacher?	He *shall* (determination).
Will you promise to come?	We *will* come (promise).

67. Shall and Will in Dependent Clauses. In dependent clauses which are introduced by *that*, expressed or understood, the auxiliary should be used which would be proper if the dependent clause were a principal clause. The sentence, *They assure us that they* **shall** *come*, is wrong. The direct assurance would be, *We* **will** *come*. The auxiliary, then, in a principal clause would be *will*. *Will* should, therefore, be the auxiliary in the dependent construction, and the sentence should read, *They assure us that they* **will** *come*. Further examples:

> I suppose *we shall* have to pay.
> He thinks that *you will* be able to do it.
> He has decided that *John shall* replace the book.

In all dependent clauses expressing a condition or contingency use *shall* with all subjects. Examples;

> *If he shall* go to Europe, it will be his tenth trip abroad.
> *If you shall* go away, who will run the farm?
> *If I shall* die, I shall die as an honest man.

EXERCISE 45

Justify the correct use of **shall** *and* **will** *in the following sentences:*

1. I will go if you wish.

2. I shall probably go if you wish.
3. I will have it in spite of all you can do.
4. We shall return by way of Dover.
5. We will fight it out on this line if it takes all summer.
6. I feel that I shall not live long.
7. We think we shall come to-morrow.
8. I promise you, the money shall be raised.
9. You will then go to Philadelphia.
10. You shall never hear from me again.
11. He will surely come to-morrow.
12. How shall you answer him?
13. I think I shall ride.
14. He is sure they will come.
15. He is sure that I will come.
16. Shall you be there?
17. Will he who fails be allowed to have a reexamination?
18. Will you be there?
19. Will all be there?
20. He says he shall be there.
21. He has promised that he will be there.
22. I fear that he will fail to pass.
23. We think she will soon be well.
24. We are determined that they shall pay.
25. We expect that they will bring their books.
26. I doubt that he will pay.
27. We have promised that we will do it.
28. If he shall ask, shall I refer him to you?

EXERCISE 46

*Fill the blanks in the following sentences with **shall** or **will**:*

1. I think I —— find the work easy.

2. I —— probably be refused, but I —— go anyway.

3. —— you be busy to-night? Yes, I —— be in class until ten.

4. I —— probably fail to pass the examination.

5. If no one assists me, I —— drown.

6. No. I —— never sell my library.

7. If I fail I —— be obliged to take an examination.

8. —— my men begin work to-day?

9. —— you stop at Chicago on your way West? No, I don't, think I ——.

10. —— you promise me to sing at the concert to-night? Yes, I —— sing to-night.

11. —— I put more wood on the fire?

12. I —— be lost; no one —— help me.

13. It —— be there when you need it.

14. It is demanded that the pupils —— be orderly and attentive.

15. I think it —— rain soon.

16. We —— be disappointed.

17. —— we be permitted to go?

18. We —— do it for you.

19. —— I go or remain at home?

20. I —— be very grateful to you if you —— do this.

21. If you —— ask her, she —— go with you.

22. If you —— stop, I —— go with you.

23. Where —— we join you?

24. I think we —— be there in time.

25. I —— go to the river for a boat ride.

26. When —— you be twenty years of age?

27. —— we ever see you again?

- 79 -

28. Perhaps we —— return next year.
29. We promise, we —— return.
30. You —— probably suffer for it.
31. I —— not impose on you in that way.
32. —— I ask for your mail?
33. I hope that we —— be there before the curtain rises.
34. —— they probably be there?
35. —— you please fetch me a paper?
36. —— we stop for you on our way downtown?
37. When —— I find you in your office?
38. They —— never do it if I can help.
39. You —— do as I say.
40. I —— never, never, go there again.
41. We —— decide what to do about that at our next meeting which —— be in October.
42. —— it make any difference to you?
43. —— I go with you?
44. No, you —— please stay here.
45. He —— never enter this house again.
46. It is believed that they —— probably be present.
47. He fears that he —— die.
48. He requests that you —— come to-day at seven o'clock.
49. She asks that it —— be sent at once.
50. It is thought that his death —— not seriously change things.
51. It is believed that the emperor —— have to retract.
52. A story is told that —— gain little credence.
53. I fear that I —— take cold.
54. She says that I —— take cold.

55. They say that they —— do it in spite of anything done to prevent.

56. He is determined that he —— go away.

57. She is determined that he —— go to school.

58. They say they —— probably not go.

59. John thinks he —— probably live to be past sixty.

60. He tells me that he thinks that he —— be elected.

61. They say that they —— meet you.

62. They assure us that we —— find good stores in Berlin.

63. He says he fears he —— miss his train.

64. Wright says his father —— become famous.

65. He writes that he —— be here to-day.

66. Do you say that you —— be present?

67. The book says that —— be wrong.

68. Does she say that she —— come?

69. I told you that I —— not come.

70. I tell you that she —— not come.

71. He says that he —— go as a matter of duty.

72. John says that —— not happen anyway.

73. Does he say that he —— surely come?

74. Does John write what he —— promise to do in the matter?

75. —— you be sure to be there?

EXERCISE 47

Write five sentences in which **shall** *is used in an independent clause, and five in which* **shall** *is used in a dependent clause.*

Write five sentences in which **will** *is used in an independent clause, and five in which* **will** *is used in a dependent clause.*

Write five interrogative sentences in which **shall** *is used and five in which* **will** *is used.*

68. Should and Would. *Should* and *would* are the past tenses of *shall* and *will*, and have corresponding uses. *Should* is used with *I* and *we*, and *would* with other subjects, to express mere futurity or probability. *Would* is used with *I* and *we*, and *should* with other subjects, to express conditional promise or determination on the part of the speaker. Examples:

Futurity:

> I *should* be sorry to lose this book.
> If we *should* be afraid of the storm, we *should* be foolish.
> It was expected that they *would* be here.

Volition or determination:

> If it *should* occur, we *would* not come.
> It was promised that it *should* not occur again.
> He decided that it *should* be done.

Should is sometimes used in the sense of *ought*, to imply duty; as, *He should have gone to her aid.*

Would is often used to indicate habitual action; as, *This would often occur when he was preaching.*

EXERCISE 48

*Justify the correct use of **should** and **would** in the following sentences:*

1. I feared that they would not come.
2. He should know his duty better than that.
3. I should be displeased if he would act that way.
4. We should be ruined if we did that.
5. You should have seen his face.
6. We would often take that road.
7. He said that he would come at once.
8. If that should happen, we should not come.
9. If you were I, what should you do?
10. I should see the president of the class.
11. We should have been at the meeting.
12. He said that we should have been at the meeting.
13. He promised that he would be at the meeting.
14. If I should say so, he would dislike me.
15. Should he come, I would go with him.

16. They would usually stop at the new hotel.

17. What would they do in the city?

18. She asked if she should write the letter.

19. She said they would write the letter.

20. She agreed that it would be right.

21. She assured us that she would attend to it.

EXERCISE 49

*Fill in the blanks with **should** or **would** in the following sentences:*

1. I fear I —— be drowned if I —— go swimming.

2. I —— be much pleased to meet him.

3. It was feared that they —— not accept.

4. If it —— storm, we —— not start.

5. She —— often come to class with no books.

6. I believed that he —— come late.

7. He —— never have been invited.

8. If that had become known, we —— surely have been ruined.

9. To think that he —— do such a thing!

10. I —— like to see the game.

11. You —— not enjoy it.

12. —— you like to see the game?

13. —— I bring my opera glasses?

14. Mary —— never have known it.

15. He —— have easily deceived her.

16. They were anxious that we —— not miss the train.

17. If we —— come late, —— it make any difference?

18. If they had proposed it, we —— have voted it down.

19. On what date —— that come?

20. I suppose I —— have done it; but, it —— have inconvenienced me.

- 83 -

21. Had Lee known that, he —— never have surrendered.

22. I —— never have believed she —— do such a thing.

23. We —— never have come.

24. —— you think him capable of such a trick?

25. I knew I —— not be here on time.

26. —— they dare to attempt opposition?

27. How —— you go about it?

28. Lincoln, under those circumstances, —— probable not have been elected.

29. It —— have changed our whole history.

30. He said that it —— have changed our whole history.

31. He said he —— come.

32. She thinks they —— not do it.

33. We believe that we —— like to go at once.

34. They say it —— be done now.

35. I think I —— like to go.

EXERCISE 50

Write five sentences in which **should** *is used independently, and five in which* **should** *is used dependently.*

Write five sentences in which **would** *is used independently, and five in which* **would** *is used dependently.*

Write five sentences in which **should** *is used in questions, and five in which* **would** *is used in questions.*

69. Use of May and Might, Can and Could. *May*, with its past tense, *might*, is properly used to denote permission. *Can*, with its past tense, *could*, refers to the ability or possibility to do a thing. These two words are often confused.

EXERCISE 51

Fill the blanks in the following sentences:

1. —— I go home?

2. —— we get tickets at that store?

3. —— the mountain be climbed?
4. —— we come into your office?
5. You —— stay as long as you wish.
6. —— you finish the work in an hour?
7. How —— you say such a thing?
8. Several people —— use the same book.
9. We —— afford to delay a while.
10. —— John go with me?
11. You —— often hear the noise.
12. What —— not be done in a week?
13. That —— be true, but it —— not be relied on.
14. What —— he do to prevent it?
15. When —— we hand in the work?

70. Participles and Gerunds. The past participle has already been mentioned as one of the principal parts of the verb. Generally, the **participles** are those forms of the verb that **are used adjectively**; as, *seeing, having seen, being seen, having been seen, seen, playing, having played,* etc. In the following sentences note that the verb form in each case modifies a substantive: *He,* ***having been invited to dine****, came early, John,* ***being sick****, could not come.* The verb form in all these cases is called a participle, and must be used in connection with either a nominative or objective case of a noun or pronoun.

The **Gerund** is the same as the participle in its forms, but differs in that, while the participle is always used adjectively, the **gerund is always used substantively**; as, *I told* ***of his winning*** *the race,* ***After his asserting*** *it, I believe the statement.*

71. Misuses of Participles and Gerunds.

1. A participle should not be used unless it stands in a grammatical and logical relation to some substantive that is present in the sentence. Failure to follow this rule leads to the error known as the "dangling participle." It is wrong to say, *The dish was broken,* ***resulting*** *from its fall,* because *resulting* does not stand in grammatical relation to any word in the sentence. But it would be right to say, *The dish was broken as a result of its fall.* Examine, also, the following examples:

Wrong: I spent a week in Virginia, *followed* by a week at Atlantic City.

Right: I spent a week in Virginia, *following* it by a week at Atlantic City.

Right: I spent a week in Virginia, *and then* a week at Atlantic City.

2. A participle should not stand at the beginning of a sentence or principal clause unless it belongs to the subject of that sentence or clause. Compare the following:

Wrong: Having been sick, it was decided to remain at home.

Right: Having been sick, I decided to remain at home.

3. A participle preceded by *thus* should not be used unless it modifies the subject of the preceding verb. Compare the following:

Wrong: He had to rewrite several pages, *thus causing* him a great deal of trouble.

Right: He had to rewrite several pages, *and was thus caused* a great deal of trouble.

Right: He had to rewrite several pages, *thus experiencing* a great deal of trouble.

4. The gerund is often used as the object of a preposition, and frequently has a noun or pronoun modifier. Owing to confusion between the gerund and the participle, and to the failure to realize that the gerund can only be used substantively, the objective case of a modifying noun or pronoun is often wrongly used before the gerund. A substantive used with the gerund should always be in the possessive case. Say, *I heard **of John's coming***, not, *I heard **of John coming***.

5. When a gerund and a preposition are used, the phrase should be in logical and immediate connection with the substantive it modifies, and the phrase should never introduce a sentence unless it logically belongs to the subject of that sentence. Exception: When the gerund phrase denotes a general action, it may be used without grammatical connection to the sentence; as, *In traveling, good drinking water is essential.* Compare the following wrong and right forms:

Wrong: *After seeing his mistake*, a new start was made.

Right: *After seeing his mistake*, he made a new start.

Wrong: *By writing rapidly, the work* can be finished.

Right: *By writing rapidly, you* can finish the work.

Wrong: *In copying the exercise*, a mistake was made.

Right: *In copying the exercise*, I made a mistake.

EXERCISE 52

In the following sentences, choose the proper form of the substantive from those italicized:

1. He spoke of *John John's* coming down.
2. The idea of *his him* singing is absurd.
3. Do you remember *me my* speaking about it?
4. What is the use of *you your* reading that?
5. *He his him* being arrested was a sufficient disgrace.
6. *He him his* being now of age, sold the farm.
7. *He him his* selling it was very unexpected.
8. You should have heard *him his* telling the story.
9. You should have heard *his him* telling of the story.
10. To think of *them they their* having been seen there!
11. What is the object of *Mary Mary's* studying French?
12. *It its* being John was a great surprise.
13. What is the use of *them they their* talking so much?
14. *John John's* going to school takes all his evenings.
15. The beauty of *James James's* writing got him the position.
16. He had heard about *me my* coming to-day.
17. *John John's* coming was a surprise.

EXERCISE 53

Wherever participles or gerunds are improperly used in the following sentences, correct the sentences so as to avoid such impropriety. See §107 for rule as to punctuation:

1. Having assented to your plan, you try to hold me responsible.

2. He asked him to make the plans, owing to the need of an experienced architect.

3. It was decided to send his son abroad being anxious for his health.

4. On hearing that, a new plan was made.

5. Moving slowly past our window, we saw a great load of lumber.

6. Intending to go to the theater, the whole afternoon was spent in town.

7. He was taken into the firm, thus gaining an increased income.

8. Not having the lesson prepared, he told John to stay after class.

9. No letter was written for more than a week, causing considerable anxiety.

10. Expecting us to come, we disappointed him.

11. After telling me the story, I left him.

12. By reading aloud to the class, they do not gain much.

13. He had to wait several hours for the train, thus causing him to lose a great deal of valuable time.

14. After listening to his lecture for an hour he became tiresome.

15. We listened attentively to his lecture, thus showing our interest.

72. Infinitives. The Infinitives are formed by the word *to* and some part of the verb or of the verb and auxiliary. For *see* and *play* as model verbs, the infinitives are as follows:

PRESENT ACTIVE	PRESENT PASSIVE
to see	to be seen
to play	to be played
PRESENT PERFECT ACTIVE	PRESENT PERFECT PASSIVE

to have seen	to have been seen
to have played	to have been played

The word *to* is frequently omitted. In general, other verbs follow the same endings and forms as do the infinitives above.

It is necessary to know the difference between the two tenses, since the misuse of tenses leads to a certain class of errors.

73. Sequence of Infinitive Tenses. The wrong tense of the infinitive is frequently used. The following rules should be observed:

1. If the action referred to by the infinitive is of the same time or of later time than that indicated by the predicate verb, the **present infinitive** should be used.

2. When the action referred to by the infinitive is regarded as completed at the time indicated by the predicate verb, the **perfect infinitive** should be used.

Examine the following examples:

Wrong: *I should have liked to have gone.*

Right: *I should have liked to go* (same or later time).

Right: *I should like to have gone* (earlier time).

Wrong: *It was bad to have been discovered.*

Right: *It is bad to have been discovered* (earlier time).

Right: *It was bad to be discovered* (same or later time).

Right: *She did not believe her son to have committed the crime* (earlier time).

Right: *When he died, he believed himself to have been defeated for the office* (earlier time.)

EXERCISE 54

In the following sentences choose the proper form from those italicized:

1. I was sorry *to have heard to hear* of John's death.
2. Should you have been willing *to go to have gone* with us?
3. The game was intended *to be played to have been played* yesterday.

4. I intended *to write to have written* long ago.

5. He wished *to have met to meet* you.

6. I should have liked *to meet to have met* you.

7. Mary was eager *to have gone to go*.

8. Nero was seen *to have fiddled to fiddle* while Rome burned.

9. Nero is said *to have fiddled to fiddle* while Rome burned.

10. This was *to be done to have been done* yesterday.

11. They agreed *to finish to have finished* it yesterday.

12. He was willing *to sing to have sung* alone.

13. He expected *to have spoken to speak* here to-morrow.

14. The Civil War is said *to cause to have caused* more loss of life than any other war.

15. Blackstone is said *to have failed to fail* at the practice of law.

16. It would have been hard *to accomplish to have accomplished* that result.

17. He was foolish enough *to have spoiled to spoil* six negatives.

18. I wanted *to have attended to attend* the convention.

19. It would be terrible *to be lost to have been lost* in the forest.

20. We were asked *to have waited to wait*.

21. I am eager *to have seen to see it*.

22. I am pleased *to meet to have met* you.

74. Split Infinitives. In the sentence, care should be taken to avoid as much as possible the inserting of an adverb or an adverbial modifier between the parts of the infinitive. This error is called the "split infinitive." Compare the following:

Bad: He seemed *to easily learn*.

Good: He seemed *to learn easily*.

Bad: He is said *to have rapidly run* along the street.

Good: He is said *to have run rapidly* along the street.

Exercise 55

Correct the following split infinitives:

1. She is known to have hurriedly read the note.
2. Mary tried to quickly call help.
3. He was asked to slowly read the next paragraph.
4. John attempted to rudely break into the conversation.
5. The plan was to secretly destroy the documents.
6. His policy was to never offend.
7. He wished to in this way gain friends.
8. He proposed to greatly decrease his son's allowance.

75. Agreement of Verb in Clauses. In a compound predicate, the parts of the predicate should agree in tense; **past tense should follow past tense, and perfect tense follow perfect tense.** Examine the following:

Wrong: He *has tried* to do, and really *did* everything possible to stop his son.

Right: He *has tried* to do, and really *has done* everything possible to stop his son.

Right: He *tried* to do, and really *did* everything possible to stop his son.

Wrong: I *hoped* and *have worked* to gain this recognition.

Right: I *hoped* and *worked* to gain this recognition.

Right: I *have hoped* and *have worked* to gain this recognition.

EXERCISE 56

Correct the following sentences:

1. I went last week and have gone again this week.
2. I have heard of his being here, but not saw him.
3. I saw John, but I have not seen Henry.
4. He desired to see John, but has not wished to see Henry.
5. John was sent for, but has not yet arrived.
6. I endeavored to find a way of avoiding that, but have not succeeded.
7. I have never seen its superior, and, in fact, never saw its equal.

8. She has succeeded in getting his promise, but did not succeed in getting his money.

9. I hoped and have prayed for your coming.

10. I have believed and usually taught that theory.

11. I intended to and have endeavored to finish the work.

12. No one has wished to see so much and saw so little of the world as I.

13. He has gained the favor of the king and was sent to Italy.

14. We have needed you and did our best to find you.

76. Omission of the Verb or Parts of the Verb. The verb or some of its parts are often omitted. This omission sometimes makes the sentence ungrammatical or doubtful in its meaning.

I like him better than John. This sentence may have the meaning shown in either of its following corrected forms: *I like him better than John **does**,* or *I like him better than **I like** John.*

As a matter of good usage, the verb or any other part of speech should be repeated wherever its omission either makes the sentence ambiguous or gives it an incomplete sound.

Bad: *He was told to go where he ought not.*

Good: *He was told to go where he ought not to go.*

Good: *He was told to go where he should not go.*

EXERCISE 57

Correct the following sentences:

1. I admire Mary more than John.

2. I think she is older than John.

3. He should have succeeded in gaining the end he tried.

4. I asked him to do what I should not have.

5. I did what I ought not.

6. We wish him better luck than Mary.

7. We want to see him more than Henry.

8. I should hate him worse than you.

9. He wanted me to do what I didn't care to.

10. You may, as you please, do it or not.

11. She may go if she wishes or not.

12. We think of you oftener than mother.

77. Model Conjugations of the Verbs To Be and To See.

CONJUGATION OF **TO BE**

PRINCIPAL PARTS: **AM, WAS, BEEN**

INDICATIVE MODE

PRESENT TENSE

Person Singular Number	*Plural Number*
1. I *am*	We *are*
2. [*]Thou *art* (you *are*)	You *are*
3. He *is*	They *are*

[Footnote *: The forms, *thou art, thou wast, thou hast*, etc., are the proper forms in the second person singular, but customarily the forms of the second person plural, *you are, you were, you have*, etc., are used also in the second person singular. These distinct second person singular forms will be used throughout the model conjugations.]

PAST TENSE

1. I *was*	We *were*
2. Thou *wast* or *wert*	You *were*
3. He *was*	They *were*

PRESENT PERFECT TENSE

(*Have* with the past participle, *been*.)

1. I *have been*	We *have been*
2. Thou *hast been*	You *have been*
3. He *has been*	They *have been*

PAST PERFECT TENSE

(*Had* with the past participle, *been*.)

1. I *had been*   We *had been*

2. Thou *hadst been*   You *had been*

3. He *had been*   They *had been*

FUTURE TENSE

(*Shall* or *will* with the present infinitive, *be*.[*])

Person Singular Number	Plural Number
1. I *shall be*	We *shall be*
2. Thou *shalt be*	You *shall be*
3. He *shall be*	They *shall be*

[Footnote *: To determine when to use *shall* and when to use *will* in the future and future perfect tenses, see §§ **65, 66**, and **67**. In these model conjugations the forms of *shall* are given with the future and the forms of *will* with the future perfect.]

FUTURE PERFECT TENSE

(*Shall* or *will* with the perfect infinitive, *have been*.[*])

1. I *will have been*   We *will have been*

2. Thou *wilt have been*   You *will have been*

3. He *will have been*   They *will have been*

[Footnote *: See Note under Future Tense.]

SUBJUNCTIVE MODE

(Generally follows *if, though, lest, although*, etc. See §**59**.)

PRESENT TENSE

1. (If) I *be*   (If) we *be*

2. (If) thou *be*   (If) you *be*

3. (If) he *be*   (If) they *be*

PAST TENSE

1. (If) I *were*   (If) we *were*

2. (If) thou *were*   (If) you *were*

3. (If) he *were*   (If) they *were*

PRESENT PERFECT TENSE

(*Have*, unchanged, with the past participle, *been*.)

1. (If) I *have been*   (If) we *have been*

2. (If) thou *have been*   (If) you *have been*

3. (If) he *have been*   (If) they *have been*

PAST PERFECT TENSE

(*Had*, unchanged, with the past participle, *been*.)

Person   Singular Number   *Plural Number*

1. (If) I *had been*   (If) we *had been*

2. (If) thou *had been*   (If) you *had been*

3. (If) he *had been*   (If) they *had been*

FUTURE TENSE

(*Shall* or *will*, unchanged, with present infinitive *be*.[*])

[Footnote *: See Note to Future Indicative.]

1. (If) I *shall be*   (If) we *shall be*

2. (If) thou *shall be*   (If) you *shall be*

3. (If) he *shall be*   (If) they *shall be*

FUTURE PERFECT TENSE

(*Shall* or *will*, unchanged, with the perfect infinitive, *have been*.*)

1. (If) I *shall have been*   (If) we *shall have been*

2. (If) thou *shall have been*   (If) you *shall have been*

3. (If) he *shall have been*   (If) they *shall have been*

POTENTIAL MODE[*]

[Footnote *: The distinct potential mode is no longer used by many authorities on grammar, and the potential forms are regarded as of the indicative mode. It has, however, been thought best to use it in these model conjugations.

As to when to use the different auxiliaries of the potential mode see §§ **68** and **69**. The conjugation with *must* (or *ought to*) is sometimes called the OBLIGATIVE MODE. The conjugation with *should* or *would* is sometimes called the CONDITIONAL MODE.]

PRESENT TENSE

(*May, can*, or *must*, with the present infinitive, *be*.)

1. I *may, can*, or *must be*	We *may, can*, or *must be*
2. Thou *mayst, canst*, or *must be*	You *may, can*, or *must be*
3. He *may, can*, or *must be*	They *may, can*, or *must be*

PAST TENSE

(*Might, could, would*, or *should*, with the present infinitive, *be*.)

Person Singular Number	Plural Number
1. I *might, could, would*, or *should be*	We *might, could, would*, or *should be*
2. Thou *mightst, couldst, wouldst*, or *shouldst be*	You *might, could, would*, or *should be*
3. He *might, could, would*, or *should be*	They *might, could, would*, or *should be*

PRESENT PERFECT TENSE

(*May, can*, or *must*, with the perfect infinitive, *have been*. For forms substitute *have been* for *be* in the present potential.)

PAST PERFECT TENSE

(*Might, could, would*, or *should*, with the perfect infinitive *have been*. For forms substitute *have been* for *be* in the past potential.)

IMPERATIVE MODE[*]

[Footnote *: The imperative is the same in both singular and plural.]

Be

INFINITIVE MODE

PRESENT TENSE	PRESENT PERFECT TENSE

To be   *To have been*

PARTICIPLES

Present Tense   Perfect Tense

Being   *Having been*

GERUNDS

(Same as participles)

CONJUGATION OF **TO SEE**

Principal Parts: **SEE, SAW, SEEN**

INDICATIVE MODE

Present Tense—Active Voice

Simple

1. I *am seeing*   We *are seeing*

2. Thou *art seeing*   You *are seeing*

3. He *is seeing*   They *are seeing*

Emphatic

1. I *do see*   We *do see*

2. Thou *dost see*   You *do see*

3. He *does see*   They *do see*

Progressive

1. I *am seeing*   We *are seeing*

2. Thou *art seeing*   You *are seeing*

3. He *is seeing*   They *are seeing*

Present Tense—Passive Voice

Simple

1. I *am seen*   We *are seen*

2. Thou *art seen*   You *are seen*

3. He *is seen*   They *are seen*

Progressive

1. I *am being seen*   We *are being seen*

2. Thou *art being seen*   You *are being seen*

3. He *is being seen*   They *are being seen*

PAST TENSE—ACTIVE VOICE

Simple

1. I *saw*   We *saw*

2. Thou *sawest*   You *saw*

3. He *saw*   They *saw*

Emphatic

Person   Singular Number   Plural Number

1. I *did see*   We *did see*

2. Thou *didst see*   You *did see*

3. He *did see*   They *did see*

Progressive

1. I *was seeing*   We *were seeing*

2. Thou *wast* or *wert seeing*   You *were seeing*

3. He *was seeing*   They *were seeing*

PAST TENSE—PASSIVE VOICE

Simple

1. I *was seen*   We *were seen*

2. Thou *wast* or *wert seen*   You *were seen*

3. He *was seen*   They *were seen*

Progressive

1. I *was being seen*   We *were being seen*

2. Thou *wert* or *wast being seen*   You *were being seen*

3. He *was being seen*   They *were being seen*

PRESENT PERFECT TENSE—ACTIVE VOICE

Simple

(Substitute *seen* for *been* in the present perfect indicative of *to be*.)

Progressive

(Substitute *been seeing* for *been* in the present perfect indicative of *to be*.)

PRESENT PERFECT TENSE—PASSIVE VOICE

(Substitute *been seen* for *been* in the present perfect indicative of *to be*.)

PAST PERFECT TENSE—ACTIVE VOICE

Simple

(Substitute *seen* for *been* in the past perfect indicative of *to be*.)

Progressive

(Substitute *been seeing* for *been* in the past perfect indicative of *to be*.)

PAST PERFECT TENSE—PASSIVE VOICE

(Substitute *been seen* for *been* in the past perfect indicative of *to be*.)

FUTURE TENSE—ACTIVE VOICE

Simple

(Substitute *see* for *be* in the future indicative of *to be*.)

Progressive

(Substitute *be seeing* for *be* in the future indicative of *to be*.)

FUTURE TENSE—PASSIVE VOICE

(Substitute *be seen* for *be* in the future indicative of *to be*.)

FUTURE PERFECT TENSE—ACTIVE VOICE

Simple

(Substitute *have seen* for *have been* in the future perfect indicative of *to be*.)

Progressive

(Substitute *have been seeing* for *have been* in the future perfect indicative of *to be*.)

FUTURE PERFECT TENSE—PASSIVE VOICE

(Substitute *have been seen* for *have been* in the future perfect indicative of *to be*.)

SUBJUNCTIVE MODE

PRESENT TENSE—ACTIVE VOICE

Simple

Person	Singular Number	Plural Number
1.	(If) I *see*	(If) we *see*
2.	(If) thou *see*	(If) you *see*
3.	(If) he *see*	(If) they *see*

Emphatic

Person	Singular Number	Plural Number
1.	(If) I *do see*	(If) we *do see*
2.	(If) thou *do see*	(If) you *do see*
3.	(If) he *do see*	(If) they *do see*

Progressive

1.	(If) I *be seeing*	(If) we *be seeing*
2.	(If) thou *be seeing*	(If) you *be seeing*
3.	(If) he *be seeing*	(If) they *be seeing*

PRESENT TENSE—PASSIVE VOICE

1.	(If) I *be seen*	(If) we *be seen*
2.	(If) thou *be seen*	(If) you *be seen*
3.	(If) he *be seen*	(If) they *be seen*

PAST TENSE—ACTIVE VOICE

Simple

1. (If) I *saw*   (If) we *saw*

2. (If) thou *saw*   (If) you *saw*

3. (If) he *saw*   (If) they *saw*

Emphatic

1. (If) I *did see*   (If) we *did see*

2. (If) thou *did see*   (If) you *did see*

3. (If) he *did see*   (If) they *did see*

Progressive

1. (If) I *were seeing*   (If) we *were seeing*

2. (If) thou *were seeing*   (If) you *were seeing*

3. (If) he *were seeing*   (If) they *were seeing*

PAST TENSE—PASSIVE VOICE

1. (If) I *were seen*   (If) we *were seen*

2. (If) thou *were seen*   (If) you *were seen*

3. (If) he *were seen*   (If) they *were seen*

PRESENT PERFECT TENSE—ACTIVE VOICE

Simple

(Substitute *seen* for *been* in the present perfect subjunctive of *to be*.)

Progressive

(Substitute *been seeing* for *been* in the present perfect subjunctive of *to be*.)

PRESENT PERFECT TENSE—PASSIVE VOICE

(Substitute *been seen* for *been* in the present perfect subjunctive of *to be*.)

PAST PERFECT TENSE—ACTIVE VOICE

Simple

(Substitute *seen* for *been* in the past perfect subjunctive of *to be*.)

Progressive

(Substitute *been seeing* for *been* in the past perfect subjunctive of *to be*.)

Past Perfect Tense—Passive Voice

(Substitute *been seen* for *been* in the past perfect subjunctive of *to be*.)

Future Tense—Active Voice

Simple

(Substitute *see* for *be* in the future subjunctive of *to be*.)

Progressive

(Substitute *be seeing* for *be* in the future subjunctive of *to be*.)

Future Tense—Passive Voice

(Substitute *be seen* for *be* in the future subjunctive of *to be*.)

Future Perfect—Active Voice

Simple

(Substitute *seen* for *been* in the future perfect subjunctive of *to be*.)

Progressive

(Substitute *been seeing* for *been* in the future perfect subjunctive of *to be*.)

Future Perfect—Passive Voice

(Substitute *been seen* for the future perfect subjunctive of *to be*.)

POTENTIAL MODE

Present Tense—Active Voice

Simple

(Substitute *see* for *be* in the present potential of *to be*.)

Progressive

(Substitute *be seeing* for *be* in the present potential of *to be*.)

Present Tense—Passive Voice

Simple

(Substitute *be seen* for *be* in the present potential of *to be*.)

Past Tense—Active Voice

Simple

(Substitute *see* for *be* in the past potential of *to be*.)

Progressive

(Substitute *be seeing* for *be* in the past potential of *to be*.)

PAST TENSE—PASSIVE VOICE

(Substitute *be seen* for *be* in the past potential of *to be*.)

PRESENT PERFECT TENSE—ACTIVE VOICE

Simple

(Substitute *have seen* for *be* in the present potential of *to be*.)

Progressive

(Substitute *have been seeing* for *be* in the present potential of *to be*.)

PRESENT PERFECT TENSE—PASSIVE VOICE

(Substitute *have been seen* for *be* in the present potential of *to be*.)

PAST PERFECT TENSE—ACTIVE VOICE

Simple

(Substitute *have seen* for *be* in the past potential of *to be*.)

Progressive

(Substitute *have been seeing* for *be* in the past potential of *to be*.)

PAST PERFECT TENSE—PASSIVE VOICE

(Substitute *have been seen* for *be* in the past potential of *to be*.)

IMPERATIVE MODE

ACTIVE VOICE

Simple

see.

Emphatic

do see.

Progressive

be seeing.

PASSIVE VOICE

be seen

INFINITIVE MODE

PRESENT TENSE—ACTIVE VOICE

Simple

to see.

Progressive

to be seeing.

PRESENT TENSE—PASSIVE VOICE

Simple

to be seen

PERFECT TENSE—ACTIVE VOICE

Simple

to have seen.

Progressive

to have been seeing.

PERFECT TENSE—PASSIVE VOICE

Simple

to have been seen.

PARTICIPLES

PRESENT TENSE—ACTIVE VOICE

seeing

PRESENT TENSE—PASSIVE VOICE

being seen

PAST TENSE—PASSIVE VOICE[*]

seen

[Footnote *: There is no past participle in the active voice.]

PERFECT TENSE—ACTIVE VOICE

Simple

having seen

Progressive

having been seeing

PERFECT TENSE—PASSIVE VOICE

having been seen

GERUNDS

Present Tense—Active Voice

seeing

Present Tense—Passive Voice

being seen

Perfect Tense—Active Voice

having seen

Perfect Tense—Passive Voice

having been seen

CHAPTER VI

CONNECTIVES: RELATIVE PRONOUNS, RELATIVE ADVERBS, CONJUNCTIONS, AND PREPOSITIONS

78. Independent and Dependent Clauses. A sentence may consist of two or more independent clauses, or it may consist of one principal clause and one or more dependent clauses.

Independent clauses are joined by conjunctions; such as, *hence, but, and, although*, etc.

Dependent clauses are joined to the sentence by relative adverbs; such as, *where, when,* etc., or by relative pronouns; as, *who, what,* etc. These dependent clauses may have the same office in the sentence as nouns, pronouns, adjectives, or adverbs. (See §7.)

79. Case and Number of Relative and Interrogative Pronouns. Failure to use the proper case and number of the relative pronouns has already been touched upon (see §29), but a further mention of this fault may well be made here.

The relative pronoun has other offices in the sentence than that of connecting the dependent and principal clauses. It may serve as a subject or an object in the clause. The sentence, *I wonder **whom** will be chosen*, is wrong, because the relative here is the subject of *will be chosen*, not the object of *wonder*, and should have the nominative form *who*. Corrected, it reads, *I wonder **who** will be chosen*. Examine the following sentences:

Wrong: We know *who* we mean.

Right: We know *whom* we mean.

Wrong: You may give it to *whoever* you wish.

Right: You may give it to *whomever* you wish.

Wrong: Do you know *whom* it is?

Right: Do you know *who* it is? (Attribute complement.)

Wrong: Everybody *who were* there were disappointed. (Disagreement in number.)

Right: Everybody *who was* there was disappointed.

The relative pronoun takes the case required by the clause it introduces, not the case required by any word preceding it. Thus, the sentence, *He gave it to **who** had the clearest right*, is correct, because *who* is the subject of the verb *had*, and therefore in the nominative case. *Give it to **whomever** they name*, is right, because *whomever* is the object of *they name*.

Errors in the use of interrogative pronouns are made in the same way as in the use of the relatives. The interrogative pronoun has other functions besides making an interrogation. It serves also as the subject or object in the sentence. Care must be taken, then, to use the proper case. Say, *Whom are you looking for?* not, *Who are you looking for?*

NOTE. Some writers justify the use of *who* in sentences like the last one on the ground that it is an idiom. When, as in this book, the object is training in grammar, it is deemed better to adhere to the strictly grammatical form.

EXERCISE 58

In the following sentences, choose the proper forms from those italicized:

1. *Who whom* do you wish to see?
2. You will please write out the name of *whoever whomever* you want.
3. I saw *who whom* was there.
4. *Who whom* was it you saw?
5. *Who whom* did you see?
6. John did not know *whom who* to ask.
7. Why did he not ask *whomever whoever* was there?
8. *Who whom* can tell the difference?
9. Give it to *whoever whomever* you please.
10. None of those who *were was* wanted *was were* there.
11. The one of those who *were was* wanted was not there.
12. He is one of those fellows who *are is* always joking.
13. *Whom who* was called "The Rail Splitter?"
14. Do you not know *whom who* it was?
15. That is one of the birds that *is are* very rare.

16. One of the books which *was were* brought was one hundred years old.

17. I am not among those *who whom were was* there.

18. Only one of the men who *were was* on board survived.

19. Everyone else who *was were* there *was were* lost.

20. I am the one of the three men who *is am are* guilty.

21. He was chosen one of the four speakers who *was were* to speak on Commencement Day.

22. It was one of the books which *were was* being sought by the librarian.

23. Give it to one of the men *who whom* is found there.

24. To *who whom* did you give it?

25. It was for *whomever whoever* was present.

26. Ask *whomever whoever* is nearest the door.

80. Conjunctive or Relative Adverbs. It is better to use a ***when* clause** only in the subordinate part of the sentence, to state the time of an event. Compare the following:

Bad: He was turning the corner, when suddenly he saw a car approaching.

Good: When he was turning the corner, he suddenly saw a car approaching.

Bad: When the news of the fire came, it was still in the early morning.

Good: The news of the fire came when it was still in the early morning.

81. Do not use a ***when*** or a ***where* clause** in defining a subject or in place of a predicate noun.

Bad: Commencement is when one formally completes his school course.

Good: Commencement is the formal completion of one's school course.

Bad: Astronomy is where one studies about the stars.

Good: Astronomy is the study of the stars.

82. *So, then,* and *also,* the conjunctive adverbs, should not be used to unite coördinate verbs in a sentence unless *and* or *but* be used in addition to the adverb.

Bad: The boys' grades are low, *so* they indicate lack of application.

Good: The boys' grades are low, *and so* indicate lack of application.

Bad: He read for a while, *then* fell asleep.

Good: He read for a while, *and then* fell asleep.

Bad: I'll be down next week; *also* I shall bring Jack along.

Good: I'll be down next week; *and also* I shall bring Jack along.

EXERCISE 59

Correct the following sentences:

1. Anarchism is when one believes in no government.
2. I am studying German, also French.
3. The clock had just struck five when the cab came.
4. I shall work until nine o'clock, then I shall retire.
5. I was sick all day, so I couldn't come to the office.
6. I was going up street yesterday when unexpectedly I met Jones.
7. Death is when one ceases to live.
8. Dinner is ready, so I shall have to cease work.
9. He told half of the story, then he suddenly stopped.
10. He loves good music, also good pictures.
11. A restaurant is where meals are served.

83. Conjunctions. There are certain conjunctions, and also certain pairs of conjunctions that frequently cause trouble.

And or **but** should not be used to join a dependent clause to an independent clause; as, *It was a new valise **and** differing much from his old one*. Say instead, *It was a new valise, differing much from his old one*, or *It was a new valise, and differed very much from his old one*. Similarly, *It was a new book **which*** (not *and which*) *interested him very much*. This "and which" construction is a frequent error; *and which* should never be used unless there is more than one relative clause, and then never with the first one.

But or **for** should not be used to introduce both of two succeeding statements. Both of the following sentences are bad by reason of this error:

*He likes geometry, **but** fails in algebra, **but** studies it hard, He read all night, **for** the book interested him, **for** it was along the line of his ambition.*

Than and **as** should not be followed by objective pronouns in sentences like this: *I am as large **as him**.* The verb in these sentences is omitted. If it is supplied, the error will be apparent. The sentence would then read, *I am as large as **him** (is large).* The correct form is, *I am as large as he (is large).* Similarly, *He is taller than **I** (am tall), She is brighter than **he** (is bright).*

As may be used as either a conjunction or an adverb. *He is **as** tall **as** I.* The first *as* is an adverb, the second *as* is a conjunction. *As* is properly used as an adverb when the equality is asserted, but, when the equality is denied, *so* should be used in its place. *He is **as** old **as** I,* is correct, but the denial should be, *He is **not so** old **as** I.* After *not* do not use *as* when *as* is an adverb.

Neither, when used as a conjunction, should be followed by **nor**; as, *Neither he **nor** (not or) I can come. Neither* should never be followed by *or*.

Either, when used as a conjunction, should be followed by **or**.

84. Placing of Correlatives. The correlatives, such as *neither—nor, either—or, not only—but also,* should be placed in clear relation to similar parts of speech or similar parts of the sentence. One should not be directed toward a verb and the other toward some other part of speech.

Bad: He *not only* brought a book, *but also* a pencil.

Good: He brought *not only* a book *but also* a pencil.

Bad: He would offer *neither* reparation *nor* would he apologize.

Good: *Neither* would he offer reparation *nor* would he apologize.

Good: He would offer *neither* reparation *nor* apology.

85. The prepositions *without, except, like,* and the adverb *directly* should not be used as conjunctions.

Wrong: *Without (unless)* you attend to class-room work, you cannot pass.

Wrong: This she would not do *except (unless)* we promised to pay at once.

Wrong: I acted just *like (as)* all the others (did).

Wrong: *Directly (as soon as)* he came, we harnessed the horses.

EXERCISE 60

Correct the following sentences:

1. Mary is as old as her.

2. I read as much as him.

3. He either wore his coat or a sort of vest.

4. He walked to the next town, but did not come back, but stayed all night.

5. We are better players than them.

6. He became thoroughly under the influence of the hypnotist and doing many absurd things.

7. There we met a man named Harmon and whom we found very entertaining.

8. They work harder than us.

9. John is not as tall as you.

10. Neither John or James is as tall as you.

11. I admire Mary more than she.

12. That can't be done without you get permission from the principal.

13. He dresses just like I do.

14. Directly he came we launched the canoes.

15. This cannot be done except you are a senior.

16. Neither she nor I was present.

17. He not only had a trained pig but also a goose.

18. Mary is not as pretty as Helen.

19. The men neither interested him nor the places.

20. He has traveled more than me.

21. We like him very much, for he is very interesting, for he has traveled so much.

22. It is a good book and which has much valuable information.

23. It was a rough town and harboring many criminals.

24. He took an interest neither in studies, nor did he care for athletics.

25. He neither took an interest in studies nor athletics.

EXERCISE 61

Construct sentences in which the following words are correctly used:

When, where, than, as—as, so—as, neither—nor, not only—but also, either—or, except, like, without, directly.

86. Prepositions. Some mistakes are made in the use of prepositions. Note the following brief list of words with the appropriate prepositions to be used with each:

agree *with* a person differ *from* (person or thing) agree *to* a proposition differ *from* or *with* an opinion bestow *upon* different *from* compare *with* (to determine value) glad *of* compare *to* (because of similarity) need *of* comply *with* part *from* (a person) confide *in* (to trust in) part *with* (a thing) confide *to* (to intrust to) profit *by* confer *on* (to give) prohibit *from* confer *with* (to talk with) reconcile *to* (a person) convenient *to* (a place) reconcile *with* (a statement) convenient *for* (a purpose) scared *by* dependent *on* think *of* or *about*

Do not use prepositions where they are unnecessary. Note the following improper expressions in which the preposition should be omitted:

continue *on*	*down* until
covered *over*	inside *of*
off *of*	outside *of*
started *out*	where *to?*
wish *for* to come	remember *of*
more than you think *for*	

Do not omit any preposition that is necessary to the completeness of the sentence.

Bad: He is a dealer and shipper *of* coal.

Good: He is a dealer *in* and shipper *of* coal.

EXERCISE 62

Illustrate in sentences the correct use of each of the expressions listed under the first paragraph of §86.

Form sentences in which correct expressions are used in place of each of the incorrect expressions listed under the second paragraph of §86.

QUESTIONS FOR THE REVIEW OF GRAMMAR

Sentences, Parts of Speech, and Sentence Elements. What are the four kinds of sentences? What are the different parts of speech? Define each. What is the difference between a clause and a phrase? What is the difference between a principal clause and a subordinate clause? Illustrate. Illustrate an adverbial clause. An adjective clause. Illustrate an adverbial phrase. An adjective phrase. What is an attribute complement? Illustrate. What is an object complement? Illustrate. Illustrate and explain the difference between simple, complex, and compound sentences.

Nouns. What is the difference between singular and plural number? How is the plural of most nouns formed? Of nouns ending in *s, ch, sh, x,* or *z*? In *y*? In *f* or *fe*? In *o*? Of letters, figures, etc.? Of compound nouns? Of proper names and titles? How is the possessive case of most nouns formed? Of nouns ending in *s* or in an *s* sound? Of a compound noun or of a group of words? What is gender? How is the feminine gender formed from the masculine? What is the difference between common and proper nouns?

Pronouns. What is a pronoun? What is the antecedent of a pronoun? What is the rule for their agreement? What is meant by "person" in pronouns? Name five pronouns of each person. Name the pronouns that indicate masculine gender. Feminine. Neuter. What pronouns may be used to refer to antecedents that stand for persons of either sex? To antecedents that are collective nouns of unity? To animals? What are nouns of common gender? By what pronouns are they referred to? Should a singular or a plural pronoun be used after *everybody*? After *some one*? After *some people*? After two nouns connected by *or*? By *nor*? By *and*? What are relative pronouns? Name them. With what kind of antecedents may each be used? What is the difference between the explanatory relative and the restrictive relative? Illustrate. What is an interrogative pronoun? What pronouns may be used only in the nominative case? In the objective case? When should the nominative case be used? The objective? The possessive? May *thou* and *you* be used in the same sentence? When should *but that* be used, and when *but what*? May *them* be used adjectively? May *which* be used with a clause as an antecedent? May *which* and *that*, or *who* and *that* be used in the same sentence with the same antecedent?

Adjectives and Adverbs. Distinguish between adjectives and adverbs. Illustrate. What is comparison? What is the positive degree, the comparative, the superlative? Illustrate each. May one say, *He is the largest of* the two? Reason? *He is the larger of the three?* Reason? *He is the largest of all?* Reason? Name three adjectives which cannot be compared. May one say, *Paris is larger than any city?* Reason? *Paris is larger than all cities?* Reason? *Paris is the largest of any other city?* Reason? Is a singular or plural noun demanded by *every*? By *two*? By *various*? By *each*? With how many objects may *either* be used? *Neither*? Where should the adjective or adverb be placed in the sentence? What is meant by a double negative? Illustrate. What is its effect? What is the definite article?

Verbs. What is a verb? What is a principal verb? An auxiliary? Illustrate. What are the principal parts of a verb? Name each. With what is the s-form used? With which form can no auxiliary be used? Make a sentence using each of the principal parts of the verbs, *go, see, begin, come, drink, write.* What is a transitive verb? Illustrate. An intransitive verb? Illustrate. What is the difference between active and passive voice? Does a transitive or does an intransitive verb have both voices? Illustrate the passive voice. Distinguish between the use of *sit* and *set.* Of *lay* and *lie.* Of *rise* and *raise.* What is the general rule for the use of the subjunctive mode? In what way and where does the subjunctive of *be* differ from the indicative in its forms? How do other verbs differ in the form of the subjunctive? In what respects should a verb agree with its subject? Does the form of the subject always determine its number? What should be the guide in determining whether to use a singular or plural verb? What class of subjects may not be used with *don't, can't,* etc.? What determines whether to use a singular or a plural verb after *who, which,* and *that*? What form of the verb is used after *you*? After *they*? When are *shall* and *should* used with *I* and *we*? When with other subjects? What rule governs their use in questions. What form is used in dependent clauses introduced by *that,* expressed or understood? In contingent clauses? Distinguish the use of *may* and *might* from *can* and *could.* What is a "dangling participle"? Is it an error? May the gerund be correctly used without any grammatical connection to the rest of the sentence? As the object of a preposition is a participle or gerund used? Which is used adjectively? Which may be used in connection with a possessive substantive as a modifier? When it is dependent on another verb, in what case should the present infinitive be used? When the perfect infinitive? What is a "split infinitive"? Need the parts of a compound predicate agree in tense?

Connectives. By what are independent clauses connected? Dependent clauses? Name two conjunctive adverbs. Should a *when* clause be used in a subordinate or in the principal part of the sentence? May *so, then,* or *also* be used alone as conjunctive adverbs? May *and* or *but* be used to join a dependent clause to a principal clause? What case should follow *than* or *as*? Should *neither* be followed by *nor* or *or*?

A GENERAL EXERCISE ON GRAMMAR

EXERCISE 63

Correct such of the following sentences as are wrong. After each sentence, in parenthesis, is placed the number of the paragraph in which is discussed the question involved:

1. He likes to boast of Mary cooking. (71.)
2. It is an error and which can't be corrected. (83.)
3. He said he should come if he could. (68.)
4. Can I use your pencil? (69.)
5. If you were I, what would you do? (68.)
6. We would like to go. (68.)
7. Neither the members of the committee nor the chairman is present. (63-5.)
8. He only spoke of history, not of art. (45.)
9. Socialists don't have no use for trusts. (46.)
10. This is John's book. (13.)
11. I feared that they should not come. (68.)
12. Mother's and father's death. (15-4.)
13. Mary was eager to have gone. (73.)
14. The boys, as well as their teacher, is to be praised. (64-1.)
15. The members of Congress watch each other. (44.)
16. I fear that I will take cold. (67.)
17. Some one has forgotten their umbrella. (20.)
18. Neither of the three is well. (43.)
19. Whom do you consider to be the brighter man in the class? (29) (41.)
20. He is determined that he shall go away. (67.)
21. Neither John nor James brought their books. (22.)
22. Whom did the man say he was? (29.)

23. His clothes look prettily. (38.)

24. The play progressed smooth until the last act. (38.)

25. Henry and William is to come to-morrow. (22.)

26. This is the lesser of the two evils. (40.)

27. Do you think you will stop at Chicago? (66.)

28. I am believed to be him. (29.)

29. He sings very illy. (40.)

30. When they come to build the bridge the stream was too deep for them to work. (54.)

31. She is very discontented. (48.)

32. Iron is the most useful of all other metals. (41-3.)

33. The barrel bursted from the pressure. (54.)

34. Shall my work soon begin? (66.)

35. He is six foot tall. (42.)

36. Seeing his mistake, I was not urged further by him. (71.)

37. Will the dog bite? (66.)

38. I am believed to be he. (29.)

39. I am eager to have seen it. (73.)

40. I think it shall rain soon. (67.)

41. She showed the dish to Mary and I. (29.)

42. Mary asked her mother to wash her face. (34-4.)

43. Who did the man say he was? (29.)

44. He deserved the place, for he is well educated, for he has been through Oxford University. (83.)

45. Choose who you please. (29.)

46. It don't make any difference about that. (64-5.)

47. The pump was froze fast. (54.)

48. A boat load of fishes was the days catch. (13-12.)

49. Wagner was never too rattled to play. (48.)

50. It is him. (29.)

51. He did it hisself. (31.)

52. He eat all there was on the table. (54.)

53. He sent a chest of tea, and it was made of tin. (34-4.)

54. The murderer was hung at noon. (54.)

55. It is a queer kind of a book. (47.)

56. You may give it to whoever you wish. (32.)

57. Whoever is nominated, will you vote for him? (32.)

58. I think I will find the work easy. (67.)

59. He sent his son abroad, being anxious for his health. (71.)

60. Neither they nor Mary was there. (22.)

61. Brewer's the blacksmith's shop. (15-6.)

62. Goliath was slew by David. (54.)

63. Myself and mother are sick. (30.)

64. John is as good, if not better than she. (41-4.)

65. If anybody creates a disturbance, have the police put them out. (21.)

66. The paper was addressed to John and herself. (30.)

67. John's and William's dog. (15-4.)

68. Tell the boy and girl to come here. (47.)

69. Everybody's else mail has came. (15, 54.)

70. He knows nothing about it but that he has read in the paper. (34-6.)

71. Awake me early in the morning. (57.)

72. If he be honest, he has not shown it. (60.)

73. Either Adams or Monroe were president. (63-4.)

74. Washington, the general and the president, was born on February 22d. (47.)

75. Horne's and Company's Store. (15-4.)

76. A hole had been tore in the ships' side. (54.)

77. I sat my chair by the window. (57.)

78. I sat myself down to rest. (57.)
79. I can't hardly see to write. (46.)
80. John is one of the people who comes each night. (64-4.)
81. He laid on the couch all day. (57.)
82. Death is when one ceases to live. (81.)
83. I was told to set here. (57.)
84. Iron is more useful than any other metal. (41-3.)
85. I not only told him, but also Morton. (84.)
86. McKinley was nowhere near so strenuous as Roosevelt. (40.)
87. It weighs several ton. (42.)
88. John is not as bright as Henry. (83.)
89. Germany and France's ships. (15-4.)
90. John's employer's wife's friend. (15-5.)
91. You had ought to go home. (54.)
92. This is the man who wants the ticket. (26.)
93. Which is the larger of the three? (41-1.)
94. An axe is the tool which they use. (26.)
95. It is that characteristic that makes him so disagreeable. (26.)
96. The horse which we drove, and the horse which you had last week are the same. (26, 34-5.)
97. I don't like those kind of people. (42.)
98. I do not question but what he is right. (34-6.)
99. Let him lay there. (57.)
100. My friend and me drove to Hughesville. (29.)
101. American and English grammar is alike. (63-1.)
102. William and Mary has to go to the city. (63-2.)
103. The boy, and not his parents, were wrong. (63-3.)
104. The price of meat has raised. (57.)

105. This train runs slow. (38.)

106. Which is the best of the two? (41-1.)

107. Iron is the most useful of all other metals. (41-3.)

108. Without the safety catch is raised, the gun can't be discharged. (85.)

109. The family is all at home. (62.)

110. The horse run the mile in two minutes. (54.)

111. This suit hasn't hardly been wore. (46, 54.)

112. The knife has laid there all day. (57.)

113. The noise of the street was very loud, which kept me awake. (34-9.)

114. The jury has agreed. (62.)

115. Such things make him terrible nervous. (38.)

116. Whom do you think is the brightest man? (29.)

117. The army were defeated. (62.)

118. If I was you, I should go at once. (60.)

119. She may go if she wishes or not. (76.)

120. Everybody whom was there was given a vote. (79.)

121. I like her better than you. (76.)

122. Who do you want? (79.)

123. Knox is one of the alumnuses of the college. (13-13.)

124. By law, no one is allowed to kill more than two deers. (13.)

125. The clock had just struck five when the cab came. (80.)

126. When was you there? (64-2.)

127. He is as tall as me. (83.)

128. Neither John nor her will come. (29.)

129. You hear such statements everywheres. (34-8, 40.)

130. You never can tell whom you will meet on the train. (79.)

131. I wish you were more like she. (29.)

132. Winter, with her frost, destroyed them all. (20.)

133. Tell everybody to cast their vote for Jones. (21.)
134. He is the only one of the members who pay dues. (64-4.)
135. Was it necessary, I should jump? (60.)
136. The production of oranges were encouraged. (64-3.)
137. The ship, with all its passengers, were lost. (64-1.)
138. He has fell from his chair. (57.)
139. I will raise and go to my father. (57.)
140. The policeman failed the ruffian with his club. (57.)
141. They make pottery in Trenton. (34-8.)
142. Iron is more useful than all metals. (41-3.)
143. I intended to and have endeavored to finish the work. (75.)
144. He won't come, except we pay his expenses. (85.)
145. Neither German or French is taught there. (83.)
146. We have needed you and did our best to find you. (75.)
147. He awoke at nine. (57.)
148. I wish I was a bird. (60.)
149. If it rains, I stay at school. (60.)
150. Thou shouldst pray when you are in trouble. (34-2.)
151. The Indians, they hid behind trees. (34-3.)
152. We started out for the city at noon. (86.)
153. The king, he said they should kill him. (34-3.)
154. Outside of the house stood a large moving van. (86.)

CHAPTER VII

SENTENCES

87. Classified as to their rhetorical construction, sentences are considered as loose, periodic, and balanced.

The **Loose Sentence** is so constructed that it may be closed at two or more places and yet make complete sense; as,

Napoleon felt his *weakness*, and tried to win back popular *favor* by concession after *concession*, until, at his fall, he had nearly restored parliamentary *government*.

Note that this sentence could be closed after the words. *weakness, favor*, and *concession*, as well as after *government*.

88. The **Periodic Sentence** holds the complete thought in suspense until the close of the sentence. Compare the following periodic sentence with the loose sentence under §87:

Napoleon, feeling his weakness, and trying to win back popular favor by concession after concession, had, at his fall, nearly restored parliamentary government.

Both loose and periodic sentences are proper to use, but, since periodic sentences demand more careful and definite thought, the untrained writer should try to use them as much as possible.

89. The **Balanced Sentence** is made up of parts similar in form, but often contrasted in meaning; as, *He is a man; Jones is a gentleman.*

90. Sentence Length. As to the length of the sentence there is no fixed rule. Frequently, sentences are too long, and are, in their thought, involved and hard to follow. On the other hand, if there is a succession of short sentences, choppiness and roughness are the result. One should carefully examine sentences which contain more than thirty or thirty-five words to see that they are clear in their meaning and accurate in their construction.

EXERCISE 64

Compose, or search out in your reading, five loose sentences, five periodic sentences, and five balanced sentences.

EXERCISE 65

In the following sentences, determine whether each sentence is loose, periodic, or balanced. Change all loose sentences to the periodic form:

1. At the same time the discontent of the artisans made the lower class fear a revolution, and that class turned to Napoleon, because they felt him to be the sole hope for order and stable government.

2. The members of the council were appointed by the king, and held office only at his pleasure.

3. A society and institutions that had been growing up for years was overturned and swept away by the French Revolution.

4. Galileo was summoned to Rome, imprisoned, and forced publicly to adjure his teaching that the earth moved around the sun.

5. He draws and sketches with tolerable skill, but paints abominably.

6. Loose sentences may be clear; periodic sentences may not be clear.

7. He rode up the mountains as far as he could before dismounting and continuing the ascent on foot.

8. They visited the town where their father had lived, and while there, procured the key to the house in which he had been born.

9. His death caused great grief and extreme financial distress in the family.

10. There stands the Tower of London in all its grimness and centuries of age, holding within its walls the scene of many a stirring tragedy.

11. Few men dislike him, but many would gladly see him overthrown merely as an example.

12. Germany is moving in the same direction, although the reformers find it a hard task to influence public opinion, and a far harder one to change the various laws prevalent in the many German states.

13. Is this thing we call life, with all its troubles, pains, and woes, after all, worth living?

14. He read much, but advanced little intellectually, for all the facts and philosophy of his reading found no permanent lodgment in his mind.

15. His coming home was very unexpected, because he had started on a trip that usually took ten days, and that he had said would take longer this time.

16. It was during the time of the National Convention that Napoleon first became very prominent by defending the convention against a mob.

EXERCISE 66

Combine each of the following groups of sentences into one well constructed long sentence:

1. In highly developed commercial communities banks cannot afford space in their vaults for valuables. Especially, they cannot afford it merely to accommodate their patrons. Hence, in such communities the furnishing of places for safe deposit has become a separate business.

2. History should be a part of the course in all schools. It develops the memory. It furnishes the explanation of many social phenomena. It broadens the intellectual view. It gives culture as no other study can give it.

3. He never desired a higher education. This was possible because of the money bequeathed to him by his father. It had left him no need for a great earning capacity. More likely, it was because of the inborn dulness and lethargy of his mind.

4. New York is the pivotal state in all national elections. Its great number of electors makes it always possible for it to throw the election either way. Therefore, until one knows to which party New York will fall, he cannot tell how the election will result.

5. Our forefathers were devout. They were easily shocked in many ways. However, they permitted many liberties in the application of sermons to particular individuals. Such things would nowadays be strongly disapproved or resented.

6. Man's life is divided into two parts by a constantly moving point. This point is called the present. It divides the past from the future.

7. The Spartans were tormented by ten thousand absurd restraints. They were unable to please themselves in the choice of their wives. They were unable to please themselves in their choice of food or clothing. They were compelled to assume a peculiar manner, and to talk in a peculiar style. Yet they gloried in their liberty.

8.	The mere approach to the temperance question is through a forest of statistics. This forest is formidable and complicated. It causes one, in time, to doubt the truth of numbers.

9.	They passed the old castle. It was almost unrecognizable. This was by reason of the scaffolding which surrounded it. The castle was now being transformed into a national museum.

10.	He stood looking with curiosity at John Peters. Peters limped slightly. Otherwise, he looked well and happy. He was moving about shaking hands right and left.

11.	They rushed at him with a yell. He had by this time reached the base of the fountain. With a sudden wonderful leap he sprang onto the railing. There he was out of reach. He balanced himself by touching the brackets which held the lamps.

12.	The unintelligent worker reminds one of the squirrel on the wheel. The squirrel rushes round and round and round all day long. At the end of the day the squirrel is still a squirrel. It is still rushing round and round. It is getting nowhere.

13.	The man looked at the ladder. He believed he could reach it. There was a sudden flash of hope in his face. His face was already scorched by the fire.

14.	Smith was financially embarrassed. He was determined to get to his home. He crawled on top of the trucks of an express car. The car was about to leave the terminal. He courted almost certain death.

15.	The commander again looks toward the hills. He looks for a long time. Something seems to excite his apprehension. He converses earnestly with the staff officer. Then the two look more than once toward a poplar tree. The tree stands at the top of the hill. Only its top half shows. The hill is on the east.

16.	The most important political question has been the tariff question. This has been most important for ten years. It is important because it is believed to have caused high prices and trusts.

17.	The pleasantest month is June. It has flowers. It has mild weather. It has a slight haze in the atmosphere. These things seem to flood one's soul with peace and contentment.

91. The essential qualities that a sentence should possess, aside from correctness, are those of Unity, Coherence, Emphasis, and Euphony.

Unity. Unity demands that the sentence deal with but one general thought, and that it deal with it in such a consistent and connected manner that the thought is clearly and effectively presented. Unity demands, also, that closely related thoughts should not be improperly scattered among several sentences.

1. Statements having no necessary relation to one another should not be embodied in one sentence.

Bad: The house sat well back from the road, *and its owner* was a married man.

Good: The house sat well back from the road. *Its owner* was a married man.

a. Avoid the "comma blunder"; that is, do not use a comma to divide into clauses what should be separate sentences, or should be connected by a conjunction.

Bad: Jones lives in the country, *he* has a fine library.

Good: Jones lives in the country. *He* has a fine library.

Good: Jones lives in the country *and has* a fine library.

b. Avoid the frequent use of the parenthesis in the sentence.

Bad: This is a city (it is called a city, though it has but twelve hundred people) that has no school-house.

2. Avoid all slipshod construction of sentences.

a. Avoid adding a clause to an apparently complete thought.

Bad: That is not an easy problem, *I think*.

Good: That, *I think*, is not an easy problem.

Good: *I do not think* that is an easy problem.

Bad: He could not be elected mayor again under any circumstances, *at least so I am told*.

Good: He could not, *I am told*, be elected mayor again under any circumstances.

Good: *I am told* that he could not under any circumstances be elected mayor again.

b. Avoid long straggling sentences.

Poor: The students often gathered to watch the practice of the team, but, just before the last game, the management excluded almost all, and only a few who had influence were allowed to enter, and this favoritism caused much hard feeling and disgust, so that the students were reluctant to support the team, and lost most of their interest, a fact which had a bad effect on the athletics of the institution.

3. Unite into one sentence short sentences and clauses that are closely and logically connected with one another.

Bad: That it is a good school is not without proof. Its diploma admits to all colleges.

Good: That it is a good school is not without proof, for its diploma admits to all colleges.

Good: That its diploma admits to all colleges is proof that it is a good school.

Bad: This fact was true of all of us. With the exception of John.

Good: This fact was true of all of us, with the exception of John.

Bad: Edward came. But John never appeared.

Good: Edward came, but John never appeared.

Bad: The town has two railroads running through it. Also, three trolley lines.

Good: The town has two railroads running through it, and also three trolley lines.

Good: The town has two railroads and three trolley lines running through it.

4. Do not change the point of view.

Bad: *We* completed our themes, and *they* were handed in to the teacher. (In the first part of the sentence, the subject is *we*; in the second it is *themes*.)

Good: We completed our themes and handed them in to the teacher.

Good: Our themes were completed and handed in to the teacher.

Bad: The *stage* took us to the foot of the hill, and *we* walked from there to the top, where *our friends* met us.

Good: *We* were taken to the foot of the hill by the stage, and *we* walked from there to the top, where *we* were met by our friends.

EXERCISE 67

Revise such of the following sentences as violate the principles of unity:

1. I frequently had ridden on a bicycle, and though the first ride made me stiff, I felt little inconvenience afterwards.

2. Of the firm Jones & Smith, Jones is a man to be respected. While Smith is thoroughly dishonest.

3. John had plenty of energy and ambition. And it is hard to understand why he didn't succeed.

4. I have taken thorough courses in history in both grade school and high school, and I also worked on the farm in the summer.

5. In the East the people are conservative. But, in the West, they are radical and progressive.

6. The news came that special rates would be given from Chicago, and that we could go to Seattle and back for fifty dollars, and so, when our checks came, we seized our grips and started on a trip which was so long and eventful, but as enjoyable as any two months we had ever spent, and gave us an experience that was very valuable in our work, which we took up on our return in the fall.

7. The town has a fine public library, besides there are a number of steel mills.

8. One may reach Boston in two ways. Either by water or by rail.

9. Women (and Christian American women, too) frequently try to evade the customs laws.

10. My aunt has some of Jefferson's silver spoons, so she says.

11. He graduated from college (I think it was Harvard, though I am not sure) and then taught for three years.

12. This is one of Hugo's novels, it is very good.

13. He accomplishes everything he undertakes, if it is at all possible.

14. Washington was president of the United States. But Hamilton guided its financial policy.

15. Every year they sell three hundred sets, and Mr. West helps to write the letters.

16. The country people were the chief patrons of the store. Although no small amount of trade came from the town.

17. The box sat under a tree, and the dog, which was a collie, would go when he was told and sit on it, and no one could call him away but his master who was very often cruelly slow in doing so, but the dog never lost patience.

18. He was one of those persons (of whom there are so painfully many) who never do what they promise.

19. He then went to his room, which was in the back of the house, to sleep, and his books were found there the next day.

20. He was the man that I had mentioned, who had been recommended for the position. Who had been refused because of his deficiencies in English.

21. I can't go, I don't think.

22. He was a very big and very strong man. And, he should have made a great football player.

23. He will surely be elected, I haven't any fear.

24. The food was good, and the service was fine, but we did not care to stay on account of the weather, which was rainy most of the time, and because it was an out-of-the-way place.

25. He converses intelligently and pleasantly, and never gossips, hence he is an agreeable companion.

26. He died of smallpox, and was ninety years old.

27. There were twenty boys in the class. Each past twenty-five years of age.

28. He is in every way honorable, at least so far as money matters are concerned.

29. I had not previously thought of going to college, but now I was enthusiastic on the matter, and all my time (at least most of it) was devoted to poring over catalogues, of which I had a great number, and many of which I knew by heart from having gone

over them so often, and finally a college was selected which seemed to suit me, so I went there in the fall to study chemistry.

30. He was very sensitive. So that we could tease him very little without making him angry.

31. There are a great number of stations along this short line of railroad, these, however, do little business.

32. They stopped and asked us the road to Milton, and it was discovered that they were going in the wrong direction, as Milton lay south of Williamsport, and we were camping twenty miles north.

33. He will most likely be suspended, it may perhaps be.

34. That day my cousin went home, and the next day John came to spend a few hours with me, and in the afternoon we drove all over the valley, but neither of us grew tired, because there were so many things to converse about, and so many long treasured questions to ask, and John left in the evening, and then I went to bed.

35. He has been proved a gambler, there you have it all.

36. Mrs. Smith (whose husband had been killed by a falling beam in one of the buildings he was constructing) consented to give us a room and board.

37. He read his lesson carefully, then he closed the book to think it over.

38. He is the most peculiar person I ever met—in the last few years at least.

39. I am reading a book, it is very interesting.

40. They get a great deal of amusement when he is walking (which he does every nice day) by whistling in time with his steps.

41. He gave me this book which you see, and I have been able to get a vast amount of information out of it.

42. It was noticed by everyone that he always behaved well. When he was in school.

43. The magician was present. And pleased everybody with his performances.

44. Because he liked music, John was considered an odd fellow, and his father was dead.

92. Coherence. Coherence in the sentence demands that the arrangement and the construction of the sentence be clear and free from ambiguity.

1. Frame the sentence so that it can have but one possible meaning.

Wrong: He owned several dogs and was greatly troubled with the mange.

Right: He owned several dogs and was greatly troubled *because they had* the mange.

Right: He was greatly troubled because several of *his dogs had* the mange.

2. See that the antecedent of every pronoun is clear and explicit.

Wrong: The dog was bitten on the front *foot which* has since died.

Right: The *dog, which* has since died, was bitten on the front foot.

Right: The dog was bitten on the front foot and has since died.

3. See that the word to which each modifier refers is unmistakable.

a. Place every modifying element as near as possible to the word which it modifies.

Wrong: He was sitting in a chair reading a *book made* in the mission style.

Right: He was sitting in a *chair made* in the mission style and was reading a book.

Right: He was sitting reading a book in a chair made in the mission style.

Wrong: The table had been inlaid by his *father, containing* over fifteen hundred pieces.

Right: The *table, containing* over fifteen hundred pieces, had been inlaid by his father.

Right: The table contained over fifteen hundred pieces and had been inlaid by his father.

b. Avoid the "squinting construction." By this term is meant the placing of a clause so that it is impossible to tell whether it refers to the preceding or succeeding part of the sentence.

Wrong: It would be hard to explain, *if you were to ask me*, what the trouble was.

Right: If you were to ask me what the trouble was, it would be hard to

explain.

4. Place correlatives so that there can be no doubt as to their office. *Neither—nor, both—and*, etc., are frequently not placed next to the expressions they are meant to connect. See §84.

Wrong: He *neither* brought a trunk *nor* a suit-case.

Right: He brought *neither* a trunk *nor* a suit-case.

Wrong: He *not only* received money from his father, *but also* his mother.

Right: He received money *not only* from his father, *but also* from his mother.

Right: He *not only* received money from his father, *but also* received it from his mother.

5. Omit no word that is not accurately implied in the sentence.

Wrong: The man *never has*, and *never will* be successful.

Right: The man *never has been*, and *never will be* successful.

Wrong: It *is no* concern to him.

Right: It *is of no* concern to him.

6. Use a summarizing word, in general, to collect the parts of a long complex sentence.

Republicans, Democrats, Socialists, Prohibitionists, and Populists—*all* were there.

7. Express similar thoughts, when connected in the same sentence, in a similar manner.

Bad: I decided *on doing* the work that night, and *to write* it out on the typewriter.

Good: I decided *to do* the work that night and *to write* it out on the typewriter.

Bad: *Textbooks are going* out of use in the modern law schools, but some schools still use them.

Good: *Textbooks are going* out of use in the modern law schools, but in some *they* are still used.

Good: Though *textbooks are going* out of use in modern law schools, *they are still used* in some of them.

Bad: *One* should never try to avoid work in school, for *you* always increase your trouble by doing so.

Good: *One* should never try to avoid work in school, for *one* always increases his trouble by doing so.

Good: *One* usually only increases *his* troubles by trying to avoid work in school.

EXERCISE 68

Point out and correct any lack of coherence that exists in the following sentences:

1. Chicken lice are troubling all the farmers in the state.
2. The statute requires that one study three years, and that you pass an examination.
3. He is home.
4. Rich and poor, old and young, large and small, good and bad, were in the assemblage.
5. He both presented me with a gold piece and an increase in salary.
6. Tell the doctor, if he comes before seven, to call.
7. When the dog came on the porch, feeling playful, I laid aside my paper.
8. I only knew John.
9. The cart was pulled by a man creaking under a heavy load.
10. John told his father that his coat was too tight for him.
11. I not only knew the president but also the whole board of directors.
12. The boxes were full of broken glass with which we made fire.
13. Mrs. Smith wants washing.
14. A young woman died very suddenly last Sunday while I was away from home as a result of a druggist's mistake.
15. He was hit in the discharge of his duty by a policeman.
16. A dog has been found by Mrs. Jones with one black ear.

17. In taking the census innumerable errors are made, thus making the result unreliable.

18. It was a pleasure to see them work and their good nature.

19. The boy went to the teacher and told him that his trouble was that he used the wrong book.

20. John was not punished because of his ill health, and he was not entirely to blame for it.

21. They said they saw them coming before they saw them.

22. The officers arrested the men and they were then locked up.

23. You made the same mistake that you now make last week.

24. Wishing to make no mistake the boy was told by him to see the professor.

25. It resulted opposite to that in which it was expected.

26. They are required to report both on their way to work and coming home.

27. Under his direction we were taught grammar and something of composition was taken up.

28. Taking all precautions, a watchman is on duty every night.

29. We tried to study, but didn't do any.

30. I do not care either to see you or Henry.

31. He has a number of kennels with many dogs scattered over the farm.

32. Mrs. X. wants a picture of her children painted very badly.

33. One of the drawbacks to the work is that time is very scarce, in this way limiting what can be done.

34. The bicycle was easy to learn to ride, which I did.

35. Rails are placed along the sides of the bridges, and horses are forbidden to trot over them.

36. John told Henry that he thought he needed help.

37. He has to stop for rest, and to avoid getting too far ahead.

38. Board, room, clothes, laundry, and amusements, are higher there than here.

39. Mathematics is not only necessary, but also languages.

40. After having read the proof, it is rolled up, and you mail it back to the printer.

41. The baskets were unpacked and the girls waited upon them.

42. They knew all that was to be learned, including John.

43. We could say that the greater part of us had both seen the Niagara Falls and Canada.

44. Let him wear a loose shoe that has sore feet.

45. Being out of work, and as I did not wish to loaf, I started to school.

46. He tried to study unsuccessfully, and in the end failed.

47. He built a house for his wife with seven windows.

48. He sent her an invitation to go for a ride on the back of his business card.

49. I saw five automobiles the other night sitting on our front door step.

50. Mrs. Smith was killed last night while cooking in a dreadful manner.

51. Post cards are both increasing in variety and beauty.

52. He neither told John nor his father.

53. Mary told her mother, if she were needed, she would be called.

54. He bought a horse when ten years old.

55. The child the parent often rebuked.

56. Sitting on a chair the entire house could be watched.

57. Coming along the road a peculiar noise was heard by us.

58. Under the enforced sanitary laws people ceased to die gradually.

59. I knew him as a physician when a boy.

60. He came leading his dog on a bicycle.

61. When wanted he sent me a letter.

93. Emphasis. Emphasis demands that the sentence be so arranged that the principal idea shall be brought into prominence and the minor details subordinated.

1. Avoid weak beginnings and weak endings in the sentence.

Bad: He was a student who did nothing right *as a rule*.

Good: He was a student, who, *as a rule*, did nothing right.

2. A change from the normal order often makes a great change in emphasis.

Normal: A lonely owl shrieked from a thick tree not far back of our camp.

Changed: From a thick tree not far back of our camp a lonely owl shrieked.

3. Where it is suitable, arrange words and clauses so as to produce a climax; i. e., have the most important come last.

Bad: Human beings, dogs, cats, horses, all living things were destroyed.

Good: Cats, dogs, horses, human beings, all living things were destroyed.

4. Avoid all words which add nothing to the thought.

Bad: He is universally praised by all people.

Good: He is universally praised.

Bad: The darkness was absolutely impenetrable, and not a thing could be seen.

Good: The darkness was absolutely impenetrable.

Bad: Mr. Smith bids me say that he regrets that a slight indisposition in health precludes his granting himself the pleasure of accepting your invitation to come to your house to dine.

Good: Mr. Smith bids me say that he regrets that sickness prevents his accepting your invitation to dine.

EXERCISE 69

Reconstruct all of the following sentences that violate the principles of emphasis:

1. Children, women, and men were slain without pity.
2. I'll prove his guilt by means of marked money, if I can.

3. Most of the students have done good work, although some have not.

4. Will you please start up the machine.

5. Where ignorance leads to a condition of blissful happiness, it would be folly to seek a condition of great wisdom.

6. A man having foolishly tried to board a moving train yesterday, was killed by being run over.

7. As a maker of violins he has never had an equal before nor since.

8. All his friends were collected together.

9. The field was so wet that we could not play on it, except occasionally.

10. Few were superior to him as a sculptor.

11. Railway companies, trolley companies, cable companies, and even hack lines were affected by the change.

12. Books were his constant companions, and he was with them always.

13. That great, gaunt mass of stones, rock, and earth, which falls upon your vision at the edge of the horizon of your view, is known by the appellation of Maxon Mountain.

14. The noise of trains is heard ceaselessly from morning till night, without stopping at all.

15. He tried to do right so far as we know.

16. That knowledge is the important thing to gain beyond all else.

94. Euphony. Euphony demands that the sentence be of pleasing sound.

1. Avoid repeating the same word in a sentence.

Bad: He *commanded* his son to obey his *commands*.

2. Avoid words and combinations of words that are hard to pronounce.

Bad: He seized quickly a thick stick.

3. Avoid a rhyme and the repetition of a similar syllable.

Bad: They went for a *walk* in order to *talk*.

EXERCISE 70

Correct such of the following sentences as lack euphony:

1. In the problems, he solved one once.
2. Most of the time he does the most he can.
3. She worries about what to wear wherever she goes.
4. It is impossible for one to believe that one so changeable can be capable of such work.
5. Those are our books.
6. Every time there was a chance for error, error was made.
7. It is true that the man spoke truly when he said, "Truth is stranger than fiction."
8. The well must have been well made, else it would not have served so well.
9. Everything he said was audible throughout the auditorium.
10. He acted very sillily.
11. He is still worried over the ill fulfillment of John's promise.
12. In his letters there is something fine in every line.
13. They ordered the members of the order to pay their dues.

EXERCISE 71. A GENERAL EXERCISE ON SENTENCES

Revise the following sentences. In parentheses after each sentence is the number of the paragraph in which the error involved is set forth:

1. Not only should we go to church, but also prayer-meeting. (92-4.)
2. In the East, just above the horizon, Mars may be readily seen in the evenings. (93-1.)
3. There is nothing distinctive about the style of the book, and it tells the story of a young Russian couple. (91-1.)
4. The nasal noise in his enunciation was displeasing. (94-2.)
5. Books, papers, records, money, checks, and receipts, were burned. (92-6.)
6. I tried to learn to write plainly, and have failed. (92-7.)
7. He has not and never will succeed in doing that. (92-5.)

8.   He is sick as a result of the picnic, it may be. (91-2.)

9.   Finally they stepped from the boat into the water, and tried to move it by all of them pushing. (92-2.)

10.   One is sure to become dull in mind, and ill in health, if you fail to exercise. (93-1.)

11.   The trip was comparatively quickly and easily made. (94-1.)

12.   She was of ordinary family, but he didn't think of criticizing that, since his own parents were of the German peasantry. (91-4.)

13.   The man was sentenced to either be hanged or life-imprisonment. (92-7.)

14.   People of wealth (and it is by no means an exception to the rule) fail to notice the misery about them. (91-1-b.)

15.   There one can see miles and miles. For there are no mountains. (91-3-a.)

16.   She told her that she thought that she had come too soon. (92-2.)

17.   By the judge's mistake, he was made a free man, and started on a career of crime again. (93-1.)

18.   Flora Macdonald was a genuine heroine. (94-3.)

19.   No criticism was made of the object, but of the means. (92-5.)

20.   If you observe the relation of spelling to pronunciation, you will have little trouble in pronunciation. (94-1.)

21.   He threw the stone at the window. And then he ran. (91-3.)

22.   The reading of Poe's stories at least is entertaining, if not elevating. (92-3-b.)

23.   John the lion killed. (92-3-b.)

24.   He arose suddenly upsetting the table. (92-3-b.)

25.   Bridget was a faithful servant, she never failed in her duties for more than five years. (91-1-a.)

26.   Instead of six, now four years only are to be spent in college. (92-3-a.)

27. We started down the river toward Harrisburg. But we did not get very far. For a storm soon came upon us. (91-3.)

28. He says that he has the book at his home which belongs to Anderson. (92-2).

29. I secured a horse and went for a ride, and after my return, we had supper. (91-4.)

30. Two of the company were killed in the battle. The others escaped without a scratch. (91-3.)

31. Different from most persons, he will not mention to any one his faults. (92-2.)

32. Not only is the book interesting, but it is instructive also. (93-1.)

33. May not only he be satisfied with the result, but delighted. (92-4.)

34. Main Street is very long, and the hotels are on Market Street. (91-1.)

35. He saw the money passing the store which had been lost. (92-2.)

CHAPTER VIII

CAPITALIZATION AND PUNCTUATION

Rules for Capitalization

95. Capitalize all proper nouns and adjectives derived from proper nouns.

France, French, Paris, Parisian, John, etc.

96. Capitalize all titles when used with proper nouns. Capitalize, also, the titles of governmental officers of high rank even when used separately. Do not capitalize other titles when used separately.

Uncle Sam, Bishop Anselm, Professor Morton, the Postmaster General, Postmaster Smith of Kelley Cross Roads, the postmaster of Kelley Cross Roads.

97. Capitalize the important words in titles of books.

The Master of Ballantrae, The Trail of the Lonesome Pine, The Discovery of America.

98. Capitalize the first word of every sentence, of every line of poetry, and of every complete sentence that is quoted.

He said, "Is it I whom you seek?"

He said she was a "perfect woman, nobly planned."

99. Capitalize the words, *mother, father*, etc., when used with proper names of persons, or when used without a possessive pronoun to refer to some definite person. Capitalize also, common nouns in phrases used as proper nouns.

Father John, my Uncle John, my uncle, if Uncle writes, if my uncle writes, along the river, along the Hudson River, Madison Square.

100. Capitalize the names, *North, South, East,* and *West*, when referring to parts of the country; words used to name the Deity; the words, *Bible* and *Scriptures*; and the words *I* and *O*, but not *oh* unless it is at the beginning of a sentence.

EXERCISE 72

Secure five examples under each of the above rules, except the last.

Rules for Punctuation

101. Punctuation should not be done for its own sake, but simply to make the meaning clearer; never punctuate where no punctuation is needed.

The following rules of punctuation are generally accepted:

The Period (.)

102. Use the period after (1) every complete sentence that is not interrogative nor exclamatory; (2) after every abbreviation; and (3) after *Yes* and *No* when used alone.

The Interrogation Point (?)

103. Use the interrogation point after every direct question.

The Exclamation Point (!)

104. Use the exclamation point after every exclamatory sentence or expression.

Alas! It is too late.

Fire if you dare!

The Comma (,)

105. Use the comma after each word of a series of words that all have the same grammatical relation to the rest of the sentence, unless conjunctions are used between all of those words.

Ours is a red, white, and blue flag.

He talked, smoked, and read.

He talked and smoked and read.

Do not, however, precede the series by a comma.

Wrong: He lectures on, Tuesdays, Thursdays, and Fridays.

Right: He lectures on Tuesdays, Thursdays, and Fridays.

106. Use the comma to separate two adjectives modifying the same noun, but not if one modifies both the other adjective and the noun.

An honest, upright man.

An old colored man.

A soiled red dress.

107. Use the comma to set off non-emphatic introductory words or phrases, and participial phrases.

John, come here.

By the way, did you see Mary?

After having done this, Cæsar crossed the Rubicon.

Cæsar crossed the Rubicon, thus taking a decisive step.

108. Use the comma to set off appositive expression (see §29, Note 1), or a geographical name that limits a preceding name.

He was told to see Dr. Morton, the principal of the school.

Muncy, Pennsylvania, is not spelled the same as Muncie, Indiana.

109. Use the comma to set off any sentence element that is placed out of its natural order.

If it is possible, he will do it.

To most people, this will seem absurd.

110. Use the comma to set off slightly parenthetical remarks that are thrown into the sentence. If the break is very marked, use the dash or parenthesis.

That, if you will permit me to explain, cannot be done without permission from the police.

Two men, Chase and Arnold, were injured.

He, himself, said it.

111. Use the comma to set off explanatory or non-restrictive clauses, but not to set off restrictive clauses. (See §§ **25** and **26**.)

Mr. Gardner, who has been working in the bank, sang at the church.

But: The Mr. Gardner whom you know is his brother.

112. Use the comma to separate coördinate clauses that are united by a simple conjunction.

He can sing well, but he seldom will sing in public.

He doesn't wish to sing, and I do not like to urge him.

113. Use the comma to separate the members of a compound sentence when those members are short and closely connected in their thought.

John carried the suit-case, I the hat box, and William the umbrella.

114. Use the comma to separate dependent and conditional clauses introduced by such words as *if, when, though,* unless the connection be close.

He did not stop, though I called repeatedly.

Your solution is right in method, even if you have made a mistake in the work.

But: You are wrong when you say that.

115. Use the comma to set off short, informal quotations, unless such quotation is a word or phrase closely woven into the sentence.

William said, "Good morning"; but, "Hello," was Henry's greeting.

But: He introduced the man as "my distinguished friend."

116. Use the comma to set off adverbs and adverbial phrases; such as, *however, then, also, for example, so to speak,* etc.

Such a man, however, can seldom be found.

This sentence, for example, can be improved by changing the order.

117. Use the comma whenever for any reason there is any distinct pause in the sentence that is not otherwise indicated by punctuation, or whenever something clearly is omitted.

We want students, not boys who simply come to school.

Cæsar had his Brutus; Charles the First, his Cromwell; ...

The Semicolon (;)

118. Use the semicolon to separate the clauses of a compound sentence that are long or that are not joined by conjunctions.

He says that he shall teach for two more years; then he shall probably return to college.

119. Use a semicolon to separate the clauses of a compound sentence that are joined by a conjunction, only when it is desirable to indicate a very definite pause.

I have told you of the theft; but I have yet to tell you of the reason for it.

120. Use a semicolon to separate the parts of a compound or a complex sentence, when some of those parts are punctuated by commas.

As men, we admire the man that succeeds; but, as honest men, we cannot admire the man that succeeds by dishonesty.

Wrong: He spends his money for theatres, and dinners, and wine, and for his family he has not a cent.

Right: He spends his money for theatres, and dinners, and wine; and for his family he has not a cent.

121. Use a semicolon before certain adverbs and adverbial expressions, when they occur in the body of the sentence and are used conjunctively; such as, *accordingly, besides, hence, thus, therefore,* etc.

I do not care to see the game; besides, it is too cold.

John is sick; however, I think he will be here.

122. Use the semicolon before the expressions, *namely, as, that is,* etc., or before their abbreviations, *viz., i.e.,* etc., when they are used to introduce a series of particular terms, simple in form, which are in apposition with a general term.

At present there are four prominent political parties; namely, the Republican, the Democratic, the Prohibition, and the Socialist.

The Colon (:)

123. Use the colon after an introduction to a long or formal quotation, before an enumeration, or after a word, phrase, or sentence that constitutes an introduction to something that follows.

Mr. Royer says in his letter: "You will remember that I promised to send you a copy of my latest musical composition. I am mailing it to you to-day."

There are four essentials of a legal contract: competent parties, consideration, agreement, and legal subject matter.

124. Use the colon after the salutation of a formal letter. (See §161.)

The Dash (—)

125. Use the dash to indicate any sudden break in thought or construction.

I am pleased to meet you, Captain—what did you say your name is?

The man I met—I refer to Captain Jones—was in the naval service.

126. Use the dash in the place of the comma to set off more definitely some part of a sentence.

I was always lacking what I needed most—money.

127. Use the dash preceded by a comma before a word which sums up the preceding part of a sentence.

Democrats, Republicans, Prohibitionists, Socialists, and Populists,—*all* were there.

128. Do not use dashes where not required or in place of some other mark of punctuation.

The Parenthesis Marks ( )

129. Use the parenthesis marks only to enclose a statement that is thrown into the sentence, but is grammatically independent of it.

He belongs (at least so it is said) to every secret society in town.

130. Do not use a comma or other punctuation mark with the parenthesis marks unless it would be required even if there were no parenthesis. When other punctuation is used it should follow the parenthesis.

They sent us (as they had agreed to do) all the papers in the case.

We expect John to bring his roommate home with him (he has been very anxious to do so); but we expect no one else.

Modern usage is to avoid entirely the use of the parentheses.

The Bracket [ ]

131. Use the bracket to enclose some statement or word of the writer that is thrown into a quotation by way of explanation or otherwise.

His letter reads: "We have decided to get Mr. Howard [his cousin] to deliver the address..."

The Quotation Marks (" ")

132. Use quotation marks to enclose quotations of the exact language of another.

The Bible says, "Charity suffereth long."

133. Use single quotation marks (' ') to enclose a quotation within a quotation.

The speaker in closing said: "I can imagine no more inspiring words than those of Nelson at Trafalgar, 'England expects every man to do his duty.'"

134. If a quotation consists of several paragraphs, quotation marks should precede each paragraph and follow the last.

135. Do not use quotation marks to enclose each separate sentence of a single continuous quotation.

136. Do not use quotation marks to enclose well-known nicknames, titles of books, proverbial phrases, or to indicate one's own literary invention.

137. Examine the location of quotation marks and other punctuation in the following sentences:

Wrong: "You may do as you wish, he said, if you only wish to do right."

Right: "You may do as you wish," he said, "if you only wish to do right."

Wrong: "Can you come," she asked?

Right: "Can you come?" she asked.

The Apostrophe (')

138. Use the apostrophe to mark certain plurals and possessives. See §§ **13** and **15**.

Use the apostrophe to indicate the omission of letters.

Doesn't, Can't, What's the matter?

The Hyphen (-)

139. Use the hyphen when a word must be divided at the end of a line.

Never divide words of one syllable, nor short words; such as, *though, through, also, besides, over*, etc.

Never divide words except at the end of a syllable, and always put the hyphen at the end of the first line, not at the beginning of the second.

Wrong division: *int-end, prop-ose, superint-endent, expre-ssion*.

Proper division: *in-tend, pro-pose, superin-tendent, expres-sion*.

In writing it is good usage not to divide a word like *expression* by placing *ex* on one line and the rest of the word on the next line.

140. Use the hyphen to divide certain compound words. No rule can be given by which to determine when compounded words demand the hyphen. Only custom determines.

Always use a hyphen with *to-day, to-morrow*, and *to-night*.

EXERCISE 73

Punctuate and capitalize the following selections. For instructions as to paragraphing and the arrangement of conversation, see §§ **143** *and* **144**:

1. however father had told us not to expect good accommodations because it is a very small town

2. tomorrow if it is a clear day we will go to pittsburgh

3. will that be satisfactory was his question

4. it doesnt make any difference said she whether you come or not

5. whats the matter with you john

6. john replied i mean that poem that begins the curfew tolls the knell of parting day

7. and that day i was only a child then I travelled all alone to new york city

8. he is a member at least he claims to be of the presbyterian church

9. the author says that the hero of waterloo wellington was a general of great military training

10. buddhist brahmin mohammedan christian jewish every religion was represented

11. his letter will tell what he wants or will attempt to do so

12. you will please hand in the following sentences one three seven and nine

13. four presidents have been unitarians namely the two adams fillmore and taft

14. the verse to which you refer is as follows

the boast of heraldry the pomp of power
all that beauty all that wealth eer gave
await alike the inevitable hour
the paths of glory lead but to the grave

15. a noun is the name of something as william france book cat

16. the train leaves at eight therefore we shall have to rise at seven at latest

17. the different points discussed are these first the history of the divine right theory second the exponents of the theory and third the result of the theory

18. in the first problem divide in the second multiply

19. if the break is slight use a comma if it is more perceptible use a semicolon if it is very sharp use a period

20. william if you gear me answer

21. he told mother that he must go home at least that is what she understood

22. as noise it is an undoubted success as music it is a flat failure

23. that may be true but i still doubt it

24. separate the clauses by a comma unless the connection be close

25. even though that be true it does not prove what we want proved

26. mary said yes but helen said no

27. he is called the peerless leader

28. such a man for example was lincoln

29. if as you say it ought to be done why dont you do it

30. that too is a mistake

31. that is wool not cotton as you seem to think

32. the english are stolid the french lively

33. in that case let us have war

34. such an opinion i may say is absurd

35. alas when i had noticed my mistake it was too late

36. the house which was built by smith is on the corner of a large lot

37. he means the house that has green shutters

38. those are all good books but none of them will do

39. dickens wrote nicholas nickleby hugo les miserables thackeray henry esmond

40. he is a good student and also a great athlete

41. he gave me a red silk handkerchief

42. having assigned the lesson he left the room

43. royers address is danville illinois

44. you will find it discussed in paragraphs one two and three

45. i had classes under the president dr harris

46. moreover naxon the cashier has fled

47. oh that is what you mean is it

48. for this you will need a piece of clean white paper

49. the bible says the lord thy god is a jealous god

50. the boundary of uncle sams lands is the rio grande river

51. theodore roosevelt is not the only strenuous man in history

52. the north quickly recovered from the civil war

53. he told mother to write to my uncle about it

54. he said then why are you here

55. in that army old young and middle aged men served for their country could no longer raise a picked army

56. he was told to ask the principal professor morton

57. in the same town muncy lives smith now a respected man

58. a peasant named ali according to a good old oriental story needing badly a donkey for some urgent work decided to apply to his neighbor mehmed whose donkey ali knew to be idle in the stable that day i am sorry my dear neighbor said mehmed in reply to alis request but i cannot please you my son took the donkey this morning to the next village i assure you insisted ali i shall take the very best care of him my dear neighbor can you not take my word demanded mehmed with a show of anger i tell you the donkey is out but at this point the donkey began to bray loudly there that is the donkey braying now well said the justly indignant mehmed if you would rather take my donkeys word than my word we can be friends no longer and under no circumstances can i lend you anything.

59. a coroner was called upon to hold an inquest over the body of an italian the only witness was a small boy of the same nationality who spoke no english the examination proceeded thus where do you live my boy the boy shook his head do you speak english another shake of the head do you speak french another shake do you speak german still no answer how old are you no reply have you father and mother no reply do you speak italian the boy gave no sign well said the coroner i have questioned the witness in four languages and can get no answer it is useless to proceed the court is adjourned.

NOTE. Further exercise in punctuation may be had by copying without the marks of punctuation selections from books, and afterwards inserting the proper marks.

CHAPTER IX

THE PARAGRAPH

141. The **Paragraph** is a connected series of sentences all dealing with the development of a single topic. Where the general subject under discussion is very narrow, the paragraph may constitute the whole composition; but usually, it forms one of a number of subtopics, each dealing with some subdivision of the general subject. For each one of these subtopics a separate paragraph should be made.

The purpose of the paragraph is to aid the reader to comprehend the thought to be expressed. The paragraph groups in a logical way the different ideas to be communicated. It gives rest to the eye of the reader, and makes clearer the fact that there is a change of topic at each new paragraph.

142. Paragraph Length. There is no fixed rule governing the proper length of the paragraph, but, probably, no paragraph need be more than three hundred words in length. If the whole composition is not more than two hundred and fifty words in length, it will not often need to be subdivided into paragraphs. In a letter, paragraphing should be more frequent than in other compositions.

Paragraphing should not be too frequent. If paragraphing is too frequent, by making each minute subdivision of equal importance, it defeats its purpose of grouping ideas about some general topic.

143. Sometimes a sentence or even a part of a sentence may be set off as a separate paragraph in order to secure greater emphasis. This, however, is only using the paragraph for a proper purpose—to aid in gaining clearness.

144. Paragraphing of Speech. In a narrative, each direct quotation, together with the rest of the sentence of which it is a part, should constitute a separate paragraph. This rule should be always followed in writing a conversation. Examine the following:

A certain Scotch family cherishes this anecdote of a trip which Dr. Samuel Johnson made to Scotland. He had stopped at the house of this family for a meal, and was helped to the national dish. During the meal the hostess asked:

"Dr. Johnson, what do you think of our Scotch broth?"

"Madam," was the answer, "in my opinion it is fit only for pigs."

"Then have some more," said the woman.

The only case in which the quoted words can be detached from the remainder of the sentence is where they form the end of the sentence after some introductory words, as in the second paragraph of the example just given.

145. Indentation of the Paragraph. The first sentence of each new paragraph should be indented. See example under §144. No other sentence should be so indented.

146. The essential qualities which each paragraph should have are: Unity, Coherence, and Emphasis.

Unity. Unity requires that the paragraph should deal with only one subject, and should include nothing which does not have a direct bearing on that subject. Thus, in the following paragraph, the italicized sentence violates the principle of Unity, because, very obviously it belongs to some other paragraph:

Never did any race receive the Gospel with more ardent enthusiasm than the Irish. *St. Patrick, a zealous priest, was thought to have banished the snakes from the island.* So enthusiastic were the Irish, that, not content with the religious work in Ireland, the Irish Church sent out its missionaries to Scotland, to Germany, and to the Alps and Apennines. It founded religious houses and monasteries....

Separate paragraphs should not be made of matter which belongs together. If the ideas can all be fairly included under one general topic, unity demands that they be grouped in one paragraph. Thus, in describing the route followed in a certain journey, one should not use a separate paragraph for each step in the journey.

Wrong:

In returning to the University, I went from Pittsburgh to Cleveland.

Then I took a berth for the night on one of the lake steamers running from Cleveland to Detroit.

From Detroit I completed the journey to Ann Arbor on an early train the next morning.

If unity is to be secured, not only must all the ideas brought out in the paragraph deal with the same topic, but also, they must be developed in some consistent, systematic order. A certain point of view should be generally maintained as to tense, subject, and manner of expression.

147. How to Gain Unity. Careful thought before beginning the paragraph is necessary if unity is to be gained. The topic of the paragraph should be determined, and should be clearly indicated by a topic sentence. Usually this topic sentence should be placed near the beginning of the paragraph. The first sentence is the clearest and best place for it. The topic sentence need not be a formal statement of the subject to be discussed, but may be any sentence that shows what is to be the central idea of the paragraph.

With the topic determined, there are various ways of developing it. It may be developed by repetition; by adding details and specific instances to the general statement; by presenting proof; by illustration; or by showing cause or effect.

148. Examine the following paragraphs. Each possesses the quality of unity. The topic sentence in each case is italicized.

To rule was not enough for Bonaparte. He wanted to amaze, to dazzle, to overpower men's souls, by striking, bold, magnificent, and unanticipated results. To govern ever so absolutely would not have satisfied him, if he must have governed silently. He wanted to reign through wonder and awe, by the grandeur and terror of his name, by displays of power which would rivet on him every eye, and make him the theme of every tongue. Power was his supreme object; but power which should be gazed at as well as felt, which should strike men as a prodigy, which should shake old thrones as an earthquake, and, by the suddenness of its new creations, should awaken something of the submissive wonder which miraculous agency inspires.

From *The Character of Napoleon Bonaparte*, by Channing.

There is something in the very season of the year that gives a charm to the festivity of Christmas. At other times we derive a great portion of our pleasures from the mere beauties of Nature. Our feelings sally forth and dissipate themselves over the sunny landscape and we "live abroad and everywhere." The song of the bird, the murmur of the stream, the breathing fragrance of spring, the soft voluptuousness of summer, the golden pomp of autumn; earth with its mantle of refreshing green, and heaven with its deep delicious blue and its cloudy magnificence—all fill us with mute but exquisite delight, and we revel in the luxury of mere sensation. But in the depth of winter, when Nature lies despoiled of every charm, and wrapped in her shroud of sheeted snow, we turn our gratifications to moral sources. The dreariness and desolation of the landscape, the short gloomy days and darksome nights, while they circumscribe our wanderings, shut in also our feelings from rambling abroad, and make us more keenly disposed for the pleasures of the social circle. Our thoughts are more concentrated; our friendly sympathies more aroused. We feel more sensibly the charm of each other's society, and are brought more closely together by dependence on each other for enjoyment. Heart calleth unto heart, and we draw our pleasures from the deep wells of living kindness which lie in the quiet recesses of our bosoms; and which, where resorted to, furnish forth the pure element of domestic felicity.

From *Christmas*, by Washington Irving.

149. Coherence. Coherence demands that each paragraph shall be perfectly clear in its meaning, and that it be so constructed that it may be readily grasped by the reader. The relation of sentence to sentence, of idea to idea, must be clearly brought out. The whole fabric of the paragraph must be woven together—it must not consist of disconnected pieces.

150. How to Gain Coherence. Where vividness or some other quality does not gain coherence in the sentence, it is usually gained by the use of words or phrases which refer to or help to keep in mind the effect of the preceding sentences, or which show the bearing of the sentence on the paragraph topic. These words may be of various sorts; as, *it, this view, however, in this way*, etc. Sometimes the subject is repeated occasionally throughout the paragraph, or is directly or indirectly indicated again at the end of the paragraph.

Examine carefully the following selections. Note the italicized words of coherence, and note in each case how they aid the flow of thought from sentence to sentence, and help to keep in mind the paragraph topic.

I will give you my opinion and advice in regard to the *two books* you have named. The *first* is interesting and easy to read. *It* is, *also*, by no means lacking in the value of the information it presents. *But the second*, while it is no less interesting and equally valuable in its contents, seems to me far more logical and scholarly in its construction. *In addition to this* I think you will find it cheaper in price, by reason of its not being so profusely illustrated. *Therefore*, I should advise you to procure the *second* for your study. *Either, indeed*, will do, but since you have a choice, take the better one.

A Husbandman who had a quarrelsome family, after having tried in vain to reconcile them by words, thought he might more readily prevail by an example. *So* he called his sons and bade them lay a bundle of sticks before him. *Then having tied them* up into a fagot, he told *the lads*, one after another, to take it up and break it. *They all tried*, but tried in vain. *Then*, untying *the fagot*, he gave *them* the sticks to break one by one. *This* they did with the greatest ease. *Then* said the father: "*Thus*, my sons, as long as you remain united, you are a match for all your enemies; but differ and separate, and you are undone." *Æsop's Fables*.

Examine also the selections under §§ **205** and **206**.

151. Emphasis. The third quality which a paragraph should possess is emphasis. The paragraph should be so constituted as to bring into prominence the topic or the point it is intended to present. The places of greatest emphasis are usually at the beginning and at the end of the paragraph. In short paragraphs sufficient emphasis is generally gained by having a topic sentence at the beginning. In longer paragraphs it is often well to indicate again the topic at the end by way of summary in order to impress thoroughly on the reader the effect of the paragraph.

EXERCISE 74

The few following suggestions for practice in paragraph construction are given by way of outline. Additional subjects and exercises will readily suggest themselves to teacher or student.

These topics are intended to apply only to isolated paragraphs—"paragraph themes." As has been suggested, more latitude in the matter of unity is allowed in compositions so brief that more than one paragraph is unnecessary.

Write paragraphs:

1. Stating the refusal of a position that has been offered to you, and giving your reasons for the refusal.

2. Describing the appearance of some building. Give the general appearance and then the details.

3. Explaining how to tie a four-in-hand necktie.

4. Stating your reasons for liking or not liking some book or play.

5. Describing the personal appearance of some one of your acquaintance.

6. To prove that the world is round.

7. To prove that it pays to buy good shoes. (Develop by illustration.)

8. Showing by comparison that there are more advantages in city life than in country life.

Write paragraphs on the following subjects:

1. My Earliest Recollection.

2. The Sort of Books I Like Best.

3. Why I Like to Study X Branch.

4. My Opinion of My Relatives.

5. The Man I Room With.
6. Why I Was Late to Class.
7. What I Do on Sundays.
8. How to Prevent Taking Cold.
9. How to Cure a Cold.
10. My Best Teacher.
11. My Favorite Town.
12. Why I Go Fishing.
13. My Favorite Month.
14. What Becomes of My Matches.
15. Baseball is a Better Game than Football.
16. The View from X Building.
17. Why I Go to School.
18. My Opinion of Rainy Days.
19. My Most Useful Friend.
20. Why I Dislike Surprise Parties.
21. Why I Like to Visit at X's.
22. The Police Service of X Town.

CHAPTER X

LETTER-WRITING

NOTE TO TEACHER.—For the purpose of training in composition, in the more elementary work, letter-writing affords probably the most feasible and successful means. Letter-writing does not demand any gathering of material, gains much interest, and affords much latitude for individual tastes in topics and expression. Besides, letter-writing is the field in which almost all written composition will be done after leaving school; and so all training in school will be thoroughly useful. For this reason, it is suggested that letter-writing be made one of the chief fields for composition work.

In Exercise 75, are given a number of suggestions for letter-writing. Others will readily occur to the teacher.

THE HEADING

152. Position of Heading. In all business letters the writer's address and the date of writing should precede the letter and be placed at the upper right hand side of the sheet not less than an inch from the top. This address and date is called the **heading**. In friendly letters the parts of the heading are sometimes placed at the end of the letter on the left side a short distance below the body of the letter. This is permissible, but to place it at the beginning in all letters is more logical and customary. Never write part of the heading at the beginning and part at the end of the letter.

153. Order of Heading. The parts of the heading should be sufficient to enable the accurate addressing of a reply, and should be in the following order: (1) the street address, (2) the town or the city address, (3) the date. If all cannot be easily placed on one line, two or even three lines should be used; but, in no case, should the above order be varied. Examples:

Wrong: March 31, 1910, Red Oaks, Iowa, 210 Semple Street.

Right: 210 Semple Street, Red Oaks, Iowa, March 31, 1910.

Right: 210 Semple Street, Red Oaks, Iowa,

March 31, 1910.

Right: 210 Semple Street,

Red Oaks, Iowa,

March 31, 1910.

If only two lines are used, put the writer's address on the first line and the date on the second.

Wrong: January 19, 1910, Sharon, Pennsylvania,

The Hotel Lafayette.

Right: The Hotel Lafayette, Sharon, Pennsylvania,

January 19, 1910.

154. Punctuation of Heading. Place a period after each abbreviation that is used. In addition to this, place commas after the street address, after the town address, after the state address, and after the number of the day of the month. Place a period after the number of the year. Examine the correct address under **§153**.

155. Faults to be Avoided in Headings. Avoid the use of abbreviations in the friendly letter, and avoid their too frequent use in the business letter.

It is better to avoid abbreviating any but the longer names of states.

Avoid all such abbreviations as the following: *St.* for *Street; Ave.* for *Avenue; Apart.* for *Apartments; Chi.* for *Chicago; Phila.* for *Philadelphia.*

Wrong: Hardie Apart., Pbg., Pa.

Right: Hardie Apartments, Pittsburg, Pa.

Do not use the sign # before the street number.

Do not omit the word *Street.*

Wrong: 229 Market.

Right: 229 Market Street.

Do not write the date thus: *9/10/10.* Represent the numbers by figures, not words. See §§ **75** and **76**. Do not use *st., rd.,* etc., after the number of the day.

Wrong: 9/8/09.

Right: September 8, 1909.

Wrong: September the Ninth, Nineteen Hundred and Nine.

Right: September 9, 1909.

Wrong: March 10th, 1910.

Right: March 10, 1910.

The Inside Address

156. Position of Inside Address. In strictly commercial letters the name and the address of the person to whom the letter is being sent should come at the beginning of the letter, and should begin flush with the margin at the left side of the page, and a little below the level of the heading. The second line of the inside address should be set in a little from the margin. See model letters under §174.

In formal friendly letters and in letters of a non-commercial nature, the inside address should stand a little below the bottom of the letter at the left side of the page. In informal friendly letters the inside address may be omitted.

157. Punctuation of Inside Address. In punctuating the inside address, place a period after each abbreviation that is used. In addition to this, place a comma after the name of the addressee, a comma after the street address, if one be given, and after the name of the town or city. Place a period after the name of the state or country. Examine the correct inside address under §174.

158. Faults to be Avoided in the Inside Address. Do not omit the town, city, or state address from the inside address.

Wrong: Mr. E. P. Griffith,

    My dear Sir:

Right: Mr. E. P. Griffith.

    Muskogee, Oklahoma.

My dear Sir:

Right: Mr. E. P. Griffith.

    221 Fiji Avenue,

        Muskogee, Oklahoma.

My dear Sir:

Do not omit proper titles.

Wrong: R. R. Stolz,

  Muncy, Pennsylvania.

Right: Mr. R. R. Stolz,

  Muncy, Pennsylvania.

When two or more men are addressed, do not omit the title *Mr.*, before the name of each of the men, unless their names constitute a partnership or trading name.

Right: Jones & Smith, (*firm name*)

  New York City.

 Gentlemen:

Right: Mr. Jones and Mr. Smith, (*not a firm name*)

  New York City.

 Gentlemen:

Avoid all abbreviations of titles preceding the name except *Mr., Mrs., Messrs.*, and *Dr.* Abbreviations of titles placed after the name, such as, *Esq., D.D., A.M.*, etc., are proper.

Do not use *Mr.* and *Esq.* with the same name.

Avoid all other abbreviations except in case of a state with a very long name. In this case it is permissible to abbreviate, but it is better form to write the name in full. *United States of America* may be abbreviated to *U. S. A.*

Wrong: Merch. Mfg. Co.,

  N. Y. C.

 Gentlemen:

Right: The Merchants' Manufacturing Company.

  New York City.

 Gentlemen:

Wrong: Mr. William Shipp,

    Bangor, Me.

Dear Sir:

Right: Mr. William Shipp,

    Bangor, Maine.

Dear Sir:

Do not place a period after the title *Miss*. *Miss* is not an abbreviation.

THE SALUTATION

159. Position of Salutation. The salutation should begin flush with the margin and on the line next below the inside address. See correctly written letters under §174.

160. Form of Salutation. The salutation varies with the form of the letter and the relations between the writer and receiver of the letter. Where the parties are strangers or mere business acquaintances the most common salutations for individuals are, *Dear Sir, Dear Madam,* or *My dear Sir, My dear Madam.* For a group of persons, or for a company or a partnership, *Gentlemen, Dear Sirs, Dear Madams* or *Mesdames* are used. In less formal business letters such salutations as, *My dear Mr. Smith,* or *Dear Miss Jaekel* may be used.

In the case of informal and friendly letters, as in business and formal letters, the salutation to be used is largely a matter of taste. The following are illustrations of proper salutations for friendly letters: *My dear Doctor, Dear Cousin, Dear Cousin Albert, Dear Miss Jaekel, Dear Major, My dear Miss Smith, Dear William, Dear Friend,* etc.

It is considered more formal to prefix *My* to the salutation.

It is over formal to use simply *Sir* or *Madam* in any letter, or to use *Dear Sir* or *Dear Madam* when writing to a familiar friend.

If one uses a very familiar salutation, such as *Dear Brown, Dear John,* etc., it is better to put the inside address at the close of the letter, or to omit it.

161. Punctuation of Salutation. Punctuate the salutation with a colon, except in informal letters, when a comma may be used.

162. Faults to be Avoided in the Salutation. Use no abbreviations except *Dr., Mr., Mrs.* Do not use the abbreviation *Dr.,* when that title is used as a final word in a salutation.

Wrong: My dear Maj. Wren:

Right: My dear Major Wren:

Wrong: My dear Dr.:

Right: My dear Doctor:

Do not use a name alone as a salutation.

Wrong: Mr. W. W. Braker:

>   Will you please inform ...

Right: Mr. W. W. Braker,

>   Muncy, Pennsylvania.

  Dear Sir:

>   Will you please inform ...

In the salutation capitalize only the important nouns and the first word of the salutation.

Wrong: My Dear Sir:

Right: My dear Sir:

Wrong: My very Dear Friend:

Right: My very dear Friend:

Wrong: Dear sir:

Right: Dear Sir:

THE BODY OF THE LETTER

163. The Subject Matter of the Letter. In friendly letters much latitude is allowed in the body of the letter, but business letters should be brief and to the point. No letter, however, should be lacking in the courteous forms or in completeness.

164. Form of Body. The body of the letter usually begins on the line below the salutation and is indented the same distance from the margin as any other paragraph would be indented. See model letters under **§174**.

In commercial letters paragraph divisions are made more frequently than in other composition. Each separate point should be made the subject of a separate paragraph.

165. Faults in Body of the Letter. In letters that are intended to be complete and formal, avoid the omission of articles, pronouns, and prepositions. Avoid also expressions that are grammatically incomplete. Only in extremely familiar and hasty letters should the "telegraph style" be adopted.

Bad: Received yours of the 10th. Have had no chance to look up man. Will do so soon.

Good: I have received your letter of the tenth. I have had no chance as yet to look up the man, but I will do so soon.

Bad: Address c/o John Smith, Mgr. Penna. Tele.

Good: Address in care of John Smith, Manager of the Pennsylvania Telegraph.

Bad: In reply will say ...

Good: In reply I wish to say ...

Bad: Yours of the 10th at hand.

Good: Your letter of the 10th is at hand.

Bad: Your favor received ...

Good: We have received your letter ...

Bad: Enclose P. O. money order for $2.

Good: We enclose post office money order for two dollars, ($2).

Bad: We have read your plan. Same is satisfactory.

Good: We have read your plan, and it is satisfactory.

Avoid the use of abbreviations in the letter.

It is well to avoid the too frequent use of the pronoun *I* in the letter, though care must be taken not to carry this caution to extremes. *I*, however, should not be omitted when necessary to the completeness of the sentence. Do not try to avoid its use by omitting it from the sentence, but by substituting a different form of sentence.

There is no objection to beginning a letter with *I*.

Punctuate the letter just as carefully as any other composition.

Excepting in letters of a formal nature, there is no objection to the use of colloquial expressions such as *can't, don't*, etc.

Unless you have some clear reason to the contrary, avoid the use of expressions that have been used so much that they are worn out and often almost meaningless. Such expressions as the following ones are not wrong, but are often used when they are both inappropriate and unnecessary.

Your esteemed favor is at hand.

In reply permit me to say ...

We beg leave to advise ...

We beg to suggest ...

Thanking you for the favor, we are ...

Please find enclosed ...

In answer to your favor of the tenth ...

We take pleasure in informing you ...

In reply would say ...

We beg to acknowledge receipt of your favor ...

Awaiting your further orders, we are ...

THE CLOSE

166. Final Words. Business letters frequently close with some final words, such as, *Thanking you again for your kind assistance, I am ..., Awaiting your further orders, we are ...,* etc. These expressions are not wrong, but are often used when not at all necessary.

167. The Complimentary Close. The complimentary close should be written on a separate line near the middle of the page, and should begin with a capital letter. Appropriateness is the only guide to the choice of a complimentary close.

The following complimentary closes are proper for business letters:

Yours respectfully,   Yours very truly,

Yours truly,   Very truly yours,

The following complimentary closes are proper for friendly letters:

Yours sincerely,   Very truly yours,

Yours very truly,   Your loving son,

Yours cordially,   Affectionately yours,

168. Faults in the Close. Do not use abbreviations, such as, *Yrs. respy., yrs. try.*, etc.

169. The Signature of the Writer. The letter should be so signed as to cause no doubt or embarrassment to any one addressing a reply. The signature should show whether the writer is a man or a woman; and, if a woman, it should indicate whether she is to be addressed as *Miss* or *Mrs.* In formal letters it is customary for a woman to indicate how she is to be addressed by signing her name in the following manner:

Sincerely yours,

    Caroline Jones.

(Mrs. William Jones).

Very truly yours,

    (Miss) Matilda Stephens.

In signing a company name write first the name of the company, and after it the name of the writer. Example:

D. Appleton & Company,

    per J. W. Miller.

Miscellaneous Directions

170. In beginning the letter, place the address and date an inch and a half or two inches below the top of the page.

Leave a margin of about a half inch or more on the left side of the page. Indent the beginning of each paragraph about an inch or more beyond the margin.

In using a four-page sheet, write on the pages in their order, 1, 2, 3, 4.

In the correctly written forms of letters under **§174** observe the indentation of the lines. The first line of the inside address should be flush with the margin, the second somewhat set in. The salutation should begin flush with the margin. The body of the letter should begin on the line below the salutation, and some distance in from the margin.

THE OUTSIDE ADDRESS

171. Position of Outside Address. Place the address on the envelope so that it balances well. Do not have it too far toward the top, too close to the bottom, nor too far to one side. See addressed envelope under §173. Place the stamp squarely in the upper right-hand corner, not obliquely to the sides of the envelope.

172. Punctuation of Outside Address. Punctuation may be omitted at the end of the lines of the address. If it is used, place a period at the end of the last line, and a comma after each preceding line.

Within the lines punctuate just as you would in the inside address.

If an abbreviation ends the line, always place a period after it, whether the other lines are punctuated or not.

173. Faults in the Outside Address. Avoid the use of abbreviations except those that would be proper in the inside address or in the heading. See §§ **155** and **158**.

Do not use the sign # before the number of the street address. No letters or sign at all should be used there. See §**155**.

Compare the following forms of addresses:

Bad: Col. Wm. Point,

#200 John St.,

Trenton, N. J.

Good: Colonel William Point,

200 John Street,

Trenton,

New Jersey.

Good: Colonel William Point

200 John Street

Trenton, New Jersey

Bad: Chas. Jones,

c/o Edward Furrey,

Wilkinsburg, Pa.

Good: Mr. Charles Jones

In care of Mr. Edward Furrey

Wilkinsburg

Pennsylvania

Bad: Rev. Walter Bertin

Good: The Reverend Walter Bertin

Bad: Pres. of Bucknell Univ.

Good: For the President of Bucknell University.

Bad: Pres. of Bucknell Univ.

Good: For the President of Bucknell University.

A properly arranged address:

> Mr. Robert D. Royer,
> 201 Tenth Street,
> Danville,
> Illinois.

174. CORRECTLY WRITTEN LETTERS

200 Mead Avenue,

Wilkinsburg, Pennsylvania,

January 12, 1909.

Mr. A. M. Weaver,

Cambridge, Massachusetts.

My dear Sir:

I have received your letter of inquiry about the sale of my law books. I will say in answer that at present I have no intention of selling them.

You may, however, be able to secure what you want from H. B. Wassel, Esquire, Commonwealth Building, Pittsburg, Pennsylvania. He has advertised the sale of a rather extensive list of books.

Very truly yours,

Charles M. Howell.

Muncy, New York, January 12, 1909.

My dear Professor Morton:

We are trying to establish in the school here some permanent system of keeping students' records. I have been told that you have worked out a card method that operates successfully. If you can give me any information in regard to your method, I shall consider it a very great favor. I enclose a stamped envelope for your reply.

Very sincerely yours,

Harris A. Plotts.

Professor E. A. Morton,

Braddock, Pennsylvania.

Braddock, Pennsylvania, January 12, 1909.

My dear Mrs. Hagon:

I wish to thank you for your kind aid in securing Captain Howard to deliver one of the lectures in our course. Only your influence enabled us to get so good a man at so Iowa price.

Very sincerely,

Sylvester D. Dunlop.

173 State Street, Detroit, Michigan,

January 23, 1910.

To whom it may concern:

It gives me great pleasure to testify to the character, ability and attainments of Mr. E. J. Heidenreich. He has been a trusted personal associate of mine for more than twenty years. He may be counted upon to do successfully anything that he is willing to undertake.

Harry B. Hutchins.

My dear Walter:

I am to be in the city only a few more weeks before leaving permanently. Before I go, I should like to have you come out and take dinner with me some evening. How would next Wednesday at six o'clock suit you? If you can come at that time, will you please write or telephone to me sometime before Tuesday?

Very cordially yours,

Paul B. Vandine.

6556 Broad Street,

Philadelphia, Pennsylvania,

March 30, 1909.

The Lafayette, Philadelphia, Pennsylvania,

    March 31, 1909.

My dear Paul:

I shall be very glad to accept your invitation to take dinner with you before you take final leave of the city. The time you mention, next Wednesday evening, is entirely satisfactory to me.

I was more than pleased to receive your invitation, for the prospect of talking over old times with you is delightful.

Sincerely yours,

    Walter Powell.

Napoleon, Ohio, February 28, 1908.

The American Stove Company,

    Alverton, Pennsylvania.

Gentlemen:

With this letter I enclose a check for ten dollars, for which please send me one of your small cook stoves, of the sort listed in your catalogue on page two hundred thirty-eight.

It will be a great favor if you will hasten the shipment of this stove as much as possible, since it is urgently needed in a summer cottage that I have for rent.

Very truly yours,

    Ernest Burrows.

223 Siegel Street, New York City,

    June 5, 1910.

The Acme Tapestry Company,

    Syracuse, New York.

Dear Sirs:

Will you please send me a price list and descriptive catalogue of your tapestries and carpets?

I have been commissioned to purchase all the tapestries and carpets that may be needed for the new Young Women's Christian Association Building, on Arlington Avenue, this city. I understand that institutions of this sort are allowed a ten per cent discount by you. Will you please tell me if this is true?

Very truly yours,

        Anna R. Fleegor.

       (Mrs. C. C. Fleegor.)

                              Lewisburg, Pennsylvania, May 10, 1910.

The Merchant's Electric Wiring Company,

      Philadelphia, Pennsylvania.

Gentlemen:

I am writing to ask if you can give me employment in your work for about ten weeks beginning June 15th. I am at present taking a course in electrical engineering at Bucknell University, and am in my sophomore year., It is my plan to gain some practical experience in various sorts of electrical work during the vacations occurring in my course. This summer I want to secure practical experience in electric wiring.

If you wish references as to my character and ability, I would refer you to Mr. William R. Stevenson, Lewisburg, Pennsylvania, and to Mr. Harry E. McCormick, Superintendent of the Street Railways Company, Danville, Illinois.

Salary is a very slight object to me in this work, and I shall be willing to accept whatever compensation you may see fit to offer me.

Respectfully yours,

        Harvey H. Wilkins.

                                    Drawsburg, Ohio, May 21, 1910.

My dear Norman:

I have just heard of your good fortune and hasten to assure you of my sincere pleasure in the news. May you find happiness and prosperity in your new location. But do not forget that your old friends are still living and will always be interested in your welfare.

Your affectionate cousin,

Mary E. Johnston.

223 Holbrook Avenue, Wilkinsburg, Indiana.

November 10, 1908.

The Jefferson Life Insurance Company,

Norfolk, Virginia.

Gentlemen:

I am the holder of Policy Number 2919 in your company. In that Policy, which was taken out about ten years ago, my occupation is stated to be carpenter. Lately I have changed occupations, and am now engaged in conducting a store. If, in order to maintain the validity of my policy, the change of occupation should be recorded on your books, will you please have the proper entry made.

I should like to know if at the present time my policy has any cash surrender value, and if so, what that value is.

Very truly yours,

Arthur J. Pearse.

Bunnell Building, Scranton, Pennsylvania,

April 20, 1909.

Mr. James R. Elliot,

Germantown, Colorado.

My dear Elliot:

Will you please send me, as soon as you conveniently can, the addresses of George English, Ira S. Shepherd, and G. N. Wilkinson.

This request for addresses may lead you to think that wedding invitations are to be looked for. Your conclusion, I am happy to say, is a correct one; I expect to be married sometime in June.

Cordially your friend,

Charles R. Harris.

The Anglo-American Hotel, Vienna, Austria,

March 19, 1907.

Dear Aunt Emily:

You will no doubt be surprised when you read the heading of this letter and learn that we are now in Vienna. We had really intended, as I wrote to you, to spend the entire months of March and April in Berlin, but a sudden whim sent us on to this city.

Until we came to Vienna I had but a very vague idea of the city, and thought it a place of little interest. I was surprised to find it a place of so many beautiful buildings and beautiful streets. Still more was I surprised to find what a festive, stylish place it is. Paris may have the reputation for fashion and frivolity, but Vienna lacks only the reputation; it certainly does not lack the fashionable and frivolous air.

The other day in one of the shops here, I discovered, as I thought, a very fine miniature. I purchased it to present to you, and have already sent it by post. It ought to reach you as soon as this letter.

We have not received the usual letter from you this week, but suppose it is because we so suddenly changed our address. The necessity of forwarding it from Berlin has probably caused the delay.

Father and Mother join in sending their love to you.

Your affectionate niece,

    Mary.

Notes in the Third Person

175. It is customary and desirable to write certain kinds of notes in the third person. Such a note contains nothing but the body of the note, followed at the left side of the paper, by the time and the place of writing.

Use no pronoun but that of the third person. Never use any heading, salutation, or signature. Use no abbreviations except *Mr., Mrs.,* or *Dr.* Spell out all dates.

176. Correctly Written Notes in the Third Person.

Mrs. Harry Moore requests the pleasure of Mr. Leighou's company at dinner on Sunday, June the first, at two o'clock.

1020 Highland Street,

    Washington, Pennsylvania,

May the twenty-fifth.

The Senior Class of Bucknell University requests the pleasure of Professor and Mrs. Morton's company on Tuesday evening, June the tenth, at a reception in honor of Governor Edwin S. Stuart.

Bucknell University,

June the fifth.

Mr. Leighou regrets that a previous engagement prevents his acceptance of Mrs. Moore's kind invitation for Sunday, June the first.

110 Braddock Avenue,

May the twenty-seventh.

EXERCISE 75

Make use of some of the following suggestions for letters. Have every letter complete in all its formal parts. Fill in details according to your own fancy:

    1.   A letter to the X Express Company of your town, complaining of their delay in delivering a package to you.

    2.   A letter to a friend, thanking him for the entertainment afforded you on a recent visit to his house.

    3.   A letter to the X Book Company, inquiring what dictionary they publish, the prices, etc.

    4.   A letter to Mr. X, asking him for a position in his office, and stating your qualifications.

    5.   A letter congratulating a friend on some good fortune that has befallen him.

    6.   A letter asking a friend his opinion of some business venture that you are thinking of entering upon. Explain the venture.

    7.   A letter to your home, describing to your parents your school.

    8.   A letter to a friend, telling him of the chance meeting with some friend.

    9.   A letter to the X store ordering from them material for covering a canoe that you are building. Explain your needs.

10. A letter describing experiences which you had on your vacation.

11. A letter arranging to meet a friend at a certain place, time, etc.

12. A letter explaining how to reach your home from the railway station. Leave no doubt.

13. A letter describing some new acquaintance.

14. A letter telling some humorous story that you have recently heard.

15. A letter to a relative telling him the recent occurrences in your town.

16. A letter detailing your plans for the succeeding year.

17. A letter describing some play which you have recently attended.

18. A letter to your parents explaining to them why you failed in an examination.

19. A letter inviting a friend to visit you at a certain time.

20. A letter accepting an invitation to visit a friend.

21. A letter stating your opinions on some public question; as, prohibition, woman suffrage, etc.

22. A letter discussing the baseball prospects in your town or school.

23. A letter to the X school, inquiring about courses of study given, prices, etc.

24. A formal third person invitation to a reception given to some organization to which you belong.

25. A formal third person acceptance of such invitation.

26. A travel letter describing your visit to various places of interest.

27. A letter describing a day's outing to a friend who was unable to go with you.

28. A letter describing a house to a man who wishes to purchase it.

29. A letter to a schoolmate describing to him various events which happened at school during his absence.

30. A letter in reply to an inquiry from a friend as to what outfit he will need to take along on a prospective camping trip.

31. A letter describing to a friend the appearance and characteristics of a dog which you have lately bought.

32. A letter to your parents telling them of your boarding place, your recent visit to the theater, your meeting an old friend, your work, your new acquaintances. Arrange the topics and make the transition as smooth as possible.

33. A letter telling about an intended celebration by the school of some national holiday.

34. A letter about a lecture that you recently attended. Describe the place, occasion, lecturer, address, etc.

35. A letter telling a friend the first impression you formed of your school.

CHAPTER XI

THE WHOLE COMPOSITION

177. By the term **Whole Composition** or **Theme** is meant a composition consisting of a number of related paragraphs all dealing with one general subject, whether the composition be a narration, a description, or an exposition.

The following general principles applying to the construction of the whole composition are stated for the guidance of the inexperienced writer.

178. Statement of Subject. Care should be used in the statement of the subject. It should not be so stated as to be more comprehensive than the composition, but should be limited to cover only what is discussed. For a small essay, instead of a big subject, take some limited phase of that subject:

Too broad: *College, Photography, Picnics.*

Properly limited: *A College Education as an Aid to Earning Power, Does College Life Make Loafers? Photography as a Recreation, How Picnics Help the Doctor.*

179. The Outline. Just as in the building of a house or of a machine, if anything creditable is to be attained, a carefully made plan is necessary before entering on the construction; so in the writing of an essay or theme, there should be made some plan or outline, which will determine what different things are to be discussed, and what is to be the method of developing the discussion. By the inexperienced writer, at least, a composition should never be begun until an outline has been formed for its development. As soon as the material for the composition is in hand, the outline should be made. It should be an aid in the construction of the composition, not a thing to be derived after the composition is completed. Only by the previous making of an outline can a logical arrangement be gained, topics properly subordinated, and a suitable proportion secured in their discussion.

In the previous chapter on the paragraph the following different subtopics, were discussed:

Definition of Paragraph.	How to Secure Unity.
Length of Paragraph.	How to Secure Coherence.
The Topic Sentence.	Too Frequent Paragraphing.

Unity in the Paragraph.	Paragraphing of Speech.
Coherence in the Paragraph.	Paragraphing for Emphasis.
Examples of Unity.	Examples showing how Unity is Destroyed.
Purpose of the Paragraph.	
Emphasis in the Paragraph.	The Paragraph Theme.

If the topics had been taken up in the above irregular order, a sorry result would have been obtained. Compare the above list of topics with the following arrangement of the same topics in a logical outline.

THE PARAGRAPH

1. Its definition and purpose.
2. Its length.

   Paragraphing of speech.

   Paragraphing for emphasis.

   Too frequent paragraphing.

3. Its essential qualities.
A. Unity.

   Definition.

   Examples showing how unity is destroyed.

   How to secure unity.

   The topic sentence.

   Development of topic sentence.

   Examples showing unity.

4. B. Coherence.

   Definition.

   How to secure coherence.

   Examples showing coherence.

5. C. Emphasis.

Places of emphasis in the paragraph.

6. Practical construction of the paragraph.

7. The paragraph theme.

180. Use and Qualities of the Outline. The use of the outline is not restricted to an expository composition, as above, but is also necessary in narration and description. Usually, in a narration, the order of time in which events occurred, is the best order in which to present them, though other arrangements may frequently be followed with very good reason.

In a description different methods may be followed. Often a general description is given, and then followed by a statement of various details. Thus, in describing a building, one might first describe in a general way its size, its general style of architecture, and the impression it makes on the observer. Then more particular description might be made of its details of arrangement and peculiarities of architecture and ornamentation.

The whole object of the outline is to secure clearness of statement and to avoid confusion and repetition. To secure this end the outline should present a few main topics to which all others either lead up or upon which they depend. These topics or subtopics should all bear some apparent and logical relation to one another. The relation may be that of chronology; that of general statement followed by details; that of cause and effect; or any other relation, so long as it is a logical and natural one.

The outline should not be too minute and detailed. It should be sufficient only to cover the various divisions of the subject-matter, and to prevent the confusion of subtopics. A too detailed outline tends to make the composition stiff and formal.

The outline should have proportion. The essential features of the subject should be the main topics. Minor subjects should not be given too great prominence, but should be subordinated to the main topics.

181. The Beginning of the Composition. To choose a method of beginning a composition often causes trouble. Usually a simple, direct beginning is the best. But sometimes an introductory paragraph is necessary in order to explain the writer's point of view, or to indicate to what phases of the subject attention is to be given. Examine the following methods of beginning.

THE INDUSTRY OF LAWYER

Oddly enough, hardly any notice is taken of an industry in which the United States towers in unapproachable supremacy above all other nations of the earth. The census does not say a word about it, nor does there exist more than the merest word about it in all the literature of American self-praise.

MY CHILDHOOD FEAR OF GHOSTS

Nothing stands out more keenly in the recollection of my childhood, than the feelings of terror which I experienced when forced to go to bed without the protecting light of a lamp. Then it was that dread, indefinite ghosts lurked behind every door, hid in every clothes-press, or lay in wait beneath every bed.

THE USES OF IRON

No other metal is put to so many uses and is so indispensable as iron.

The opening sentences of a composition should be able to stand alone; their meaning or clearness should not depend upon reference to the title.

Bad:

THE VALUE OF LATIN IN THE HIGH SCHOOL

There is a rapidly growing belief *that this study* has too large a place in our high-school courses of study.

Good:

THE VALUE OF LATIN IN THE HIGH SCHOOL

There is a rapidly growing belief *that Latin* has too large a place in our high school courses of study.

182. Unity in the Composition. Unity is an essential element of the whole composition as well as of the paragraph, and its demands here are in general the same. Nothing must be brought into the composition which does not fall well within the limits of the subject. In the different subdivisions, also, nothing must be discussed which properly belongs to some other division of the topic.

As in the paragraph, a definite point of view should be adopted and adhered to. There must not be a continual changing of relation of parts of the composition to the subject, nor of the writer's relation to the subject.

A consistent point of view is especially necessary in a narrative. If the writer is telling of events within his own experience, care must be taken not to bring in any conversation or occurrence, at which, by his own story, he could not have been present. A continual changing back and forth between present and past tenses must also be avoided. One or the other should be adopted consistently.

183. Coherence in the Composition. A composition must also be coherent. Its different parts must be closely knit together and the whole closely knit to the subject. Just as in the paragraph, words of reference and transition are needed, so in the composition, words, or sentences of reference and transition are needed, in order to bind the whole together and show the relation of its parts.

For this purpose, the beginning of a new division or any definite change of topic should be closely marked, so as to prevent confusion. There should be transition sentences, or sentences which show the change of topic from paragraph to paragraph, and yet at the same time bridge the thought from paragraph to paragraph. These transition sentences may come at the end of a preceding paragraph, or at the beginning of a following one, or at both of these places.

Examine the following parts of paragraphs in which the words or phrases showing transition from part to part are italicized:

(Last sentence of first paragraph)

... The American War was pregnant with misery of every kind.

(Second paragraph)

The mischief, however, recoiled on the unhappy people of this country, who were made the instruments by which the wicked purposes of the authors were effected. The nation was drained of its best blood, and of its vital resources of men and money. The expense of the war was enormous— much beyond any former experience.

(Third paragraph)

And yet, what has the British nation received in return for this expense....

... I was now enabled to see the *extent and aspect of my prison. In its size* I had been greatly mistaken....

(Beginning of paragraph following one on Unity in the paragraph)

The second of the essentials of the paragraph, coherence, demands that....

Frequently, in the longer compositions, a separate paragraph is devoted to accomplishing the transition from part to part. Observe the following:

(Paragraph 7)

... The only other law bearing on this matter is the Act of Assembly of last year authorizing the receipts from the automobile taxes to be used in the construction of roads. This then completes the enumeration of what has already been done toward building good roads.

(Paragraph 8. Transitional paragraph)

There are, however, several promising plans for the securing of this important result, which are now being seriously discussed.

(Paragraph 9)

The first of these plans is ...

The following are a few of the words and phrases often used to indicate transition and to show relation between the paragraphs: *So much for, It remains to mention, In the next place, Again, An additional reason, Therefore, Hence, Moreover, As a result of this, By way of exception.*

Examine the selection under §187.

184. The Ending of the Composition. In a longer composition, the ending should neither be too abrupt, nor, on the other hand, should it be too long drawn out. It should be in proportion to the length of the composition. Usually, except in the case of a story, it should consist of a paragraph or two by way of summary or inference. In a story, however, the ending may be abrupt or not. The kind of ending depends entirely upon the nature and the scheme of development of the story. Examine the following endings:

Ending of a theme on *The Uses of Iron*:

Only some of the more important uses of this wonderful metal, iron, have been mentioned. There are hundreds of other uses to which it is constantly put—uses which no other metal could fill. Gold may once have been called the king of metals, but it has long since lost its claim to that title.

Ending of a story:

John heard her answer, and began to move slowly away from the gate.

"Good-bye," he said.

And then he was gone, forever.

Suggested subjects for the making of outlines and compositions.

1. How I Spent my Vacation.
2. Shall Final Examinations be Abolished?
3. The Subjects which Should be Taught in High Schools.
4. My Qualifications for a Position.
5. The Uses of Iron.
6. Paul Revere's Ride.

7. The City Park.

8. My Town as a Place of Residence.

9. The Value of Railroads.

10. Why I Believe in Local Option.

11. A Winter's Sleigh Ride.

12. Shall Foreign Immigration be Restricted?

13. My Youthful Business Ventures.

14. Why I Belong to the X Political Party.

15. Various Methods of Heating a House.

185. Below is given in full Lincoln's *Gettysburg Speech*. It is perfect in its English and its construction. Study it with especial reference to its coherence, unity, and emphasis. Some of the words of coherence have been italicized.

Fourscore and seven years ago our fathers, brought forth upon this continent a new nation, conceived in liberty, and dedicated to the proposition that all men are created equal. *Now* we are engaged in a great civil war, testing whether *that nation*, or any nation so conceived and so dedicated, can long endure.

We are met on a great battle-field of *that war.* We have come to dedicate a portion of *that field* as the final resting-place for those who here gave their lives that that nation might live. It is altogether fitting and proper that we should do *this. But* in a larger sense we cannot dedicate, we cannot consecrate, we cannot hallow this ground. The brave men, living and dead, who *struggled here* have consecrated it far above our power to add or detract. The world will little note, nor long remember, what we say here; but it can never forget what *they did here.*

It is for us, the living, *rather*, to be dedicated here to the unfinished work which *they who fought here* have thus far so nobly advanced. *It is rather for us* to be here dedicated to the great task remaining before us, that from these honored dead we take increased devotion to that cause for which they here gave the last full measure of devotion; that we here highly resolve that *these dead* shall not have died in vain; that *this nation*, under God, shall have a new birth of freedom, and that government of the people, by the people, and for the people, shall not perish from the earth.

186. *Small Economies*, from Mrs. Gaskell's *Cranford*.

I have often noticed that everyone has his own individual small economies—careful habits of saving fractions of pennies in some one peculiar direction—any disturbance of which annoys him more than spending shillings or pounds on some real extravagance.

An old gentleman of my acquaintance, who took the intelligence of the failure of a Joint-Stock Bank, in which some of his money was invested, with a stoical mildness, worried his family all through a long summer's day because one of them had torn (instead of cutting) out the written leaves of his now useless bank-book. Of course, the corresponding pages at the other end came out as well, and this little unnecessary waste of paper (his private economy) chafed him more than all the loss of his money. Envelopes fretted his soul terribly when they first came in. The only way in which he could reconcile himself to such waste of his cherished article was by patiently turning inside out all that were sent to him, and so making them serve again. Even now, though tamed by age, I see him casting wistful glances at his daughters when they send a whole inside of a half-sheet of note paper, with the three lines of acceptance to an invitation, written on only one of the sides.

I am not above owning that I have this human weakness myself. String is my foible. My pockets get full of little hanks of it, picked up and twisted together, ready for uses that never come. I am seriously annoyed if any one cuts the string of a parcel instead of patiently and faithfully undoing it fold by fold. How people can bring themselves to use india-rubber bands, which are a sort of deification of string, as lightly as they do, I cannot imagine. To me an india rubber band is a precious treasure. I have one which is not new—one that I picked up off the floor nearly six years ago. I have really tried to use it, but my heart failed me, and I could not commit the extravagance.

Small pieces of butter grieve others. They cannot attend to conversation because of the annoyance occasioned by the habit which some people have of invariably taking more butter than they want. Have you not seen the anxious look (almost mesmeric) which such persons fix on the article? They would feel it a relief if they might bury it out of their sight by popping it into their own mouths and swallowing it down; and they are really made happy if the person on whose plate it lies unused suddenly breaks off a piece of toast (which he does not want at all) and eats up his butter. They think that this is not waste.

Now Miss Matty Jenkins was chary of candles. We had many devices to use as few as possible. In the winter afternoons she would sit knitting for two or three hours—she could do this in the dark, or by firelight—and when I asked if I might not ring for candles to finish stitching my wristbands, she told me to "keep blind man's holiday." They were usually brought in with tea; but we only burnt one at a time. As we lived in constant preparation for a friend who might come in any evening (but who never did), it required some contrivance to keep our two candles of the same length, ready to be lighted, and to look as if we burnt two always. The candles took it in turns; and, whatever we might be talking or doing, Miss Matty's eyes were habitually fixed upon the candle, ready to jump up and extinguish it and to light the other before they had become too uneven in length to be restored to equality in the course of the evening.

One night, I remember this candle economy particularly annoyed me. I had been very much tired of my compulsory "blind man's holiday," especially as Miss Matty had fallen asleep, and I did not like to stir the fire and run the risk of awakening her; and so I could not even sit on the rug, and scorch myself with sewing by firelight, according to my usual custom....

187. A List of Books for Reading. These books are of a varied character and are all interesting and of recognized excellence in their English. Most of them are books that, as a matter of general education, should be read by everyone.

Fiction:

    Treasure Island—Stevenson.
    Kidnapped—Stevenson.
    Dr. Jekyll and Mr. Hyde—Stevenson.
    The Scarlet Letter—Hawthorne.
    Twice Told Tales—Hawthorne.
    The Luck of Roaring Camp—Bret Harte.
    Tales of Mystery and Imagination—Poe.
    Silas Marner—Eliot.
    Robinson Crusoe—Defoe.
    Ivanhoe—Scott.
    Henry Esmond—Thackeray.
    Pilgrim's Progress—Bunyan.
    The Spy—Cooper.
    The Man without a Country—Hale.
    Tales of a Traveller—Irving.
    The Legend of Sleepy Hollow—Irving.
    Rip Van Winkle—Irving.
    Lorna Doone—Blackmore.
    Uncle William—Lee.
    The Blue Flower—Van Dyke.

Non-fiction:

Sesame and Lilies—Ruskin.
Stones of Venice—Ruskin.
The American Commonwealth—Bryce.
A History of the English People—Green.
Views Afoot—Taylor.
The Autocrat of the Breakfast Table—Holmes.
Conspiracy of Pontiac—Parkman.
Autobiography—Franklin.
Lincoln—Douglas Debates.
Critical Periods of American History—Fiske.
Certain Delightful English Towns—Howells.
The Declaration of Independence.
Bunker Hill Oration—Webster.
On Conciliation with America—Burke.
The Sketch Book—Irving.

CHAPTER XII

WORDS.—SPELLING.—PRONUNCIATION

188. To write and to speak good English, one must have a good working vocabulary. He must know words and be able to use them correctly; he must employ only words that are in good use; he must be able to choose words and phrases that accurately express his meaning; and he must be able to spell and pronounce correctly the words that he uses.

Words

189. Good Use. The first essential that a word should have, is that it be in good use. A word is in good use when it is used grammatically and in its true sense, and is also:

(1) *Reputable*; in use by good authors and writers in general. The use of a word by one or two good writers is not sufficient to make a word reputable; the use must be general.

(2) *National*; not foreign or local in its use.

(3) *Present*; used by the writers of one's own time.

190. Offenses against Good Use. The offenses against good use are usually said to be of three classes: Solecisms, Barbarisms, and Improprieties.

191. Solecisms are the violations of the principles of grammar. Solecisms have been treated under the earlier chapters on grammar.

192. Barbarisms. The second offense against good use, a barbarism, is a word not in reputable, present or national use. The following rules may be given on this subject:

1. **Avoid obsolete words.** Obsolete words are words that, once in good use, have since passed out of general use. This rule might also be made to include obsolescent words: words that are at present time passing out of use. Examples of obsolete words:

methinks	yesterwhiles	twixt
yclept	afeard	shoon

2. **Avoid newly coined expressions or new uses of old expressions.** There are a great many words current in the newspapers and in other hasty writing that have not the sanction of general good use at the present time,

though many of these words may in time come into use. A safe rule is to avoid all words that are at all doubtful. Examples:

an invite	an exposé	a try
enthuse	a combine	fake

A common newspaper fault is the coining of a verb or adjective from a noun, or a noun from a verb. Examples:

locomote	suicided	derailment
pluralized	burglarized	refereed

3. **Avoid foreign words.** A foreign word should not be used until it has become naturalized by being in general, reputable use. Since there are almost always English words just as expressive as the foreign words, the use of the foreign words usually indicates affectation on the part of the one using them. Examples:

billet-doux (love letter)	conversazione (conversation)
ad nauseam (to disgust)	distingué (distinguished)
ad infinitum (infinitely)	entre nous (between us)

4. **Avoid provincialisms.** Provincialisms are expressions current and well understood in one locality, but not current or differently understood in another locality. Examples:

guess (think)	reckon (suppose)
near (stingy)	smart (clever)
tuckered (tired out)	lift (elevator)
tote (carry)	ruination (ruin)

5. **Avoid vulgarisms.** Vulgarisms are words whose use shows vulgarity or ignorance. Such words as the following are always in bad taste:

chaw	nigger	your'n
gal	flustrated	hadn't oughter
haint	dern	his'n

6. **Avoid slang.** Slang is a form of vulgarism that is very prevalent in its use even by educated people. Slang words, it is true, sometimes come into good

repute and usage, but the process is slow. The safest rule is to avoid slang expressions because of their general bad taste and because of their weakening effect on one's vocabulary of good words. Examples of slang:

grind	swipe	booze
long green	on a toot	dough
pinch	peach	dukes

7. **Avoid clipped or abbreviated words.** The use of such words is another form of vulgarism. Examples:

pard (partner)	rep (reputation)
doc (doctor)	cal'late (calculate)
musee (museum)	a comp (complimentary ticket)

8. **Avoid technical or professional words.** Such words are usually clearly understood only by persons of one class or profession. Examples:

valence	hagiology	allonge
kilowatt	sclerosis	estoppel

193. When Barbarisms May be Used. In the foregoing rules barbarisms have been treated as at all times to be avoided. This is true of their use in general composition, and in a measure true of their use in composition of a special nature. But barbarisms may sometimes be used properly. Obsolete words would be permissible in poetry or in historical novels, technical words permissible in technical writing, and even vulgarisms and provincialisms permissible in dialect stories.

EXERCISE 76

Substitute for each of the barbarisms in the following list an expression that is in good use. When in doubt consult a good dictionary:

Chaw, quoth, fake, reckon, dern, forsooth, his'n, an invite, entre nous, tote, hadn't oughter, yclept, a combine, ain't, dole, a try, nouveau riche, puny, grub, twain, a boom, alter ego, a poke, cuss, eld, enthused, mesalliance, tollable, disremember, locomote, a right smart ways, chink, afeard, orate, nary a one, yore, pluralized, distingué, ruination, complected, mayhap, burglarized, mal de mer, tuckered, grind, near, suicided, callate, cracker-jack, erst, railroaded, chic, down town, deceased (verb), a rig, swipe, spake, on a toot, knocker, peradventure, guess, prof, classy, booze, per se, cute, biz, bug-house, swell, opry, rep, photo, cinch, corker, in cahoot, pants, fess up, exam, bike, incog, zoo, secondhanded, getable, outclassed, gents, mucker, galoot, dub, up against it, on tick, to rattle, in hock, busted on the bum, to watch out, get left.

EXERCISE 77

Make a list of such barbarisms as you yourself use, and devise for them as many good substitute expressions as you can. Practice using the good expressions that you have made.

EXERCISE 78

Correct the italicized barbarisms in the following sentences:

1. They can go *everywheres*.
2. He spends all his time *grinding*.
3. There *ain't* a *sightlier* town in the state.
4. He ate the whole *hunk* of cake

He was treated very *illy*.

5. Smith's new house is very *showy*.
6. Not *muchly* will I go.
7. All were ready for breakfast before *sun-up*.
8. Do you like *light-complected* people?
9. I had never *orated* before.
10. Their clothes are always *tasty* in appearance.
11. He has money, but he is very *near*.
12. He left the room *unbeknown* to his mother.
13. If manners are any indication, she belongs to the *nouvea riche*.
14. I feel pretty *tollable* today.
15. I *reckon* all will be able to get seats.
16. Do you *callate* to get there before noon?
17. If I had as much *long green* as he has, I wouldn't be such *tight-wad*.
18. He was the *beau ideal* of soldier.
19. John is a *crazy cuss*.

20. Let me say *en passant* we did not ask for the tickets.
21. Even at that time John had a bad *rep*.
22. That woman is the Countess of Verdun, *née* Smith.
23. *Methinks* you are wrong.
24. The teacher *spake* sharply to her.
25. I *didn't go for to do* it.
26. It will be published *inside of* two months.
27. The duke and his wife were travelling *incog*.
28. I hadn't *thought on* that.
29. There is little difference *twixt* the two.
30. Come now, *fess up*.
31. It's a *right smart ways* to Williamsport.
32. You *wot* not what you say.
33. He bought a *poke* of apples for his lunch.
34. Brown runs a pretty *classy* store.
35. I finally *got shut* of him.
36. I *could of* jumped across.
37. That can't be done *nohow*.
38. You make such *dumb* mistakes.
39. I never saw such a *bum* show.

194. Improprieties. The third offense against good use, an impropriety, is the use of a proper word in an improper sense. In many cases an offense against good use may be called a barbarism, an impropriety, or a solecism, since the fields covered by the three terms somewhat overlap one another. Many improprieties have their origin in the similarities in sound, spelling or meaning of words. The following exercises deal with a number of common improprieties resulting from the confusion of two similar words.

Exercise 79

Study the proper use of the words given under each of the following divisions. In each group of sentences fill the blanks with the proper words:

Accept, except. See Glossary at end of book, under *except*.

1. I cannot —— your gift.

2. Have you no books —— these?

3. Cicero was not —— from the list of those condemned.

4. He —— the invitation.

Affect, effect. See Glossary under *effect*.

1. Will your plan —— a reform from the present condition?

2. The sad news will seriously —— his mother.

3. How was the bank —— by the indictment of its president?

4. The change of schedule was —— without a hitch.

Aggravate, irritate. See Glossary.

1. Her manner —— me.

2. The crime was —— by being committed in cold blood.

3. The children do everything they can to —— her.

4. His illness was —— by lack of proper food.

Allude, mention. See Glossary.

1. He —— (to) certain events which he dared not name directly.

2. The attorney —— (to) no names.

3. That passage in his book delicately —— (to) his mother.

4. In his speech the labor leader boldly —— (to) his recent arrest.

Argue, augur. *To argue* is to state reasons for one's belief. *To augur* means *to foretell, to presage.*

1. The reported quarrel —— ill for the army.

2. He will —— at length on any subject.

3. Her darkening looks —— a quarrel.

Avocation, vocation. A *vocation* is one's principal work or calling. *An avocation* is something aside from or subordinate to that principal calling.

1. The young physician enthusiastically pursues his ——.

2. Law is his ——, but politics is his ——.

3. The ministry should be one's ——, never his ——.

4. While preparing for his life work, school teaching was for a time his ———.

Besides, beside. *Besides* means *in addition to*. *Beside* refers to place; as, *He sits beside you.*

1. ——— you, who else was there?
2. Is there nothing ——— this to do?
3. John walked ——— me.
4. ——— me was a tree.

Calculate, intend. *To calculate* means *to compute, to adjust* or *to adapt*. *Intend* means *to have formed the plan to do something.*

1. He ——— to sell books this summer.
2. He ——— that the work will take ten years.
3. He ——— to finish it as soon as he can.
4. The oil is ——— to flow at the rate of a gallon a minute.

Character, reputation. See Glossary.

1. In this community his ——— is excellent.
2. One's friends may endow him with a good ———, but not with a good ———.
3. Slander may ruin one's ———, but it will not destroy his ———.
4. See that your ——— is right, and your ——— will establish itself.

Claim, assert. *To claim* means to make a demand for what is one's own. It should not be confused with *assert*.

1. I ——— that I am innocent.
2. John ——— the property as his.
3. They ——— their right to the land.
4. The cashier ——— the money in payment of a note.
5. Do you still ——— that you were born in America?

Council, counsel, consul. A *council* is a group of persons called in to hold consultation. *Counsel* means *an adviser*, as a lawyer; or *advice* that is given. *Consul* is an officer of the government.

1. In the colonies each governor had his ——.

2. The advisers gave him —— when he desired it.

3. The United States has a —— in every important foreign port.

4. In criminal cases the accused must be provided with ——.

5. The president's cabinet constitutes for him a sort of ——.

6. In Rome two —— were elected to manage the affairs of the state.

Emigration, immigration. See Glossary.

1. Foreign —— into the United States is greatly restricted.

2. The —— of the citizens of the United States to Canada is becoming a matter of concern.

3. Our —— Bureau enforces the Chinese Exclusion Act.

4. The treatment of the royalists caused a great —— from France.

Good, well. *Good* is an adjective. *Well* is usually an adverb, though sometimes an adjective; as, *Are you well to-day?*

1. She talks very ——.

2. She prepares a —— paper, even if she does not write ——.

3. Do —— what you are doing.

4. Did you have a —— time?

5. Recite it as —— as you can.

House, home. *House* means only *a building*. *Home* means a place that is one's habitual place of residence.

1. He thought often of the flowers about the door of his old ——.

2. They have recently bought a —— which they intend to make their ——.

3. Mr. Heim lives here now, but his —— is in Lewisburg.

4. He has several miserable —— that he rents.

5. Such a place is not fit to be called a ——.

Most, almost. *Almost* is an adverb meaning *nearly*. *Most* never has this meaning.

1. I was —— injured when the machine broke.
2. It is —— time for him to come.
3. The —— discouraging thing was his indifference.
4. I —— missed the car.
5. —— of the books are torn.

Let, leave. See Glossary, under *leave*.

1. Will his employer —— him go so early.
2. I shall —— at noon.
3. —— me help you with your coat.
4. —— me here for a while.
5. This book I —— with you.
6. Do not —— that danger disturb you.

Like, as. *Like* should not be used as a conjunction in the sense of *as*. As a preposition it is correct. It is wrong to say, *Do like I do*; but right to say, *Do as I do*.

1. He looks —— James.
2. Read —— James does.
3. Does she look —— me?
4. She thinks of it —— I thought.
5. Lincoln could do a thing —— that.
6. Other men could not do —— Lincoln did.

Likely, liable, probably. It is better to avoid using *likely* as an adverb; but it may be used as an adjective; as, *He is likely to come*. *Probably* refers to any sort of possibility. *Liable* refers to an unpleasant or unfavorable possibility; it should not be used as equivalent to *likely*.

1. He is —— to arrest for doing that.
2. The president's car will —— arrive at noon.
3. It is —— to rain to-day.
4. Is he —— to write to us?

    5. Continued exposure makes one more —— to serious illness.

    6. What will —— come of it?

Loan, lend. *Loan* should be used only as a noun, and *lend* only as a verb.

    1. I wish to obtain a —— of fifty dollars.

    2. Will you —— me your knife?

    3. A —— of money loses both itself and friend.

    4. A —— is something that one —— to another.

Mad, angry. Mad means *insane, uncontrollably excited through fear*, etc. It should not be used for *angry* or *vexed*.

    1. His manner of speaking makes me ——.

    2. It makes one —— to see such behavior.

    3. The noise almost drove me ——.

Much, many. *Much* refers to quantity; *many* to number.

    1. Sometimes they have as —— as fifty in a class.

    2. —— of the trouble comes from his weak eyes.

    3. Do you use —— horses on the farm?

    4. How —— marbles did the boy have?

Near, nearly. *Near* is an adjective; *nearly* an adverb.

    1. Is the work —— finished?

    2. The man was —— the end of the porch.

    3. It was —— noon when Blucher came.

    4. They are —— insane with worry.

    5. Mary is not —— so old as John.

Observation, observance. *Observation* means to *watch, to look at*. *Observance* means *to celebrate, to keep*. *Observation* applies to a fact or an object; *observance* to a festival, a holiday, or a rule.

    1. The —— of the astronomer proved the theory.

    2. Sunday —— is of value to one's bodily as well as to one's spiritual health.

    3. The —— of the sanitary regulations was insiste d upon.

4. The scientist needs highly developed powers of ——.

Respectively, respectfully. *Respectively* means *particularly, relating to each.* *Respectfully* means *characterized by high regard.*

1. These three kinds of architecture were characterized —— as "severe," "graceful," and "ornate."

2. Sign your letter "Yours ——," not "yours ——."

3. Their shares were —— two hundred dollars and five hundred dollars,

4. The class —— informed the faculty of their desire.

Suspect, expect. *Suspect* means *to mistrust.* *Expect* means *to look forward to.*

1. I —— that he will come.

2. He —— his brother of hiding his coat.

3. When do you —— to finish the work?

4. The man was never before —— of having done wrong.

Teach, learn. See Glossary under *learn.*

1. You must —— him to be careful.

2. He must —— to be careful.

3. To —— a class to study is a difficult task.

4. Who —— your class to-day.

Transpire, happen. *Transpire* does not mean *to happen.* It means *to become gradually known, to leak out.*

1. She knows everything that —— in the village.

2. It —— that he had secretly sold the farm.

3. No more important event than this has —— in the last ten years.

4. It has now —— that some money was stolen.

Quite, very. *Quite* is not in good use in the sense of *very* or *to a great degree.* It properly means *entirely.*

1. The book is —— easy to study.

2. Have you —— finished your work.

3. The train ran —— slowly for most of the distance.

4. That is —— easy to do.

5. We were —— unable to reach the city any sooner.

EXERCISE 80

The following list includes some groups of words that are often confused. For the proper meaning of the words refer to a good dictionary. Write sentences using the words in their proper senses:

practical, skilled	sensible, sensitive
couple, two	access, accession
future, subsequent	allusion, illusion, delusion
folk, family	conscience, consciousness
evidence, testimony	identity, identification
party, person, firm	limit, limitation
plenty, many, enough of	majority, plurality
portion, part	materialize, appear
solicitation, solicitude	invent, discover
human, humane	prescribe, proscribe
bound, determined	some, somewhat, something
fix, mend	mutual, common
foot, pay	noted, notorious
creditable, credible	wait for, wait on
exceptionable, exceptional	in, into

EXERCISE 81

Show how the use of each of the two italicized words in the following sentences would affect the meaning of the sentence:

1. We experienced a *succession series* of hindrances.

2. That *statement assertion* was made by an eye witness.

3. The student has remarkable *ability capacity*.

4. In my *estimate estimation* the cost will be higher than fifty dollars.

5. The *import importance* of his words is not fully understood.

6. The *union unity* of the clubs is remarkable.

7. The *acts actions* of the president were closely watched.

8. The man needed a new *stimulus stimulant*.

9. He was *captivated captured* by her unusual charms.

10. We are quick to *impute impugn* motives that we think to exist.

11. He was *convinced convicted* by John's argument.

12. The dog's suffering was *alleviated relieved* by the medicine.

13. He *persuaded advised* me to consult a lawyer.

14. His behavior was *funny odd*.

15. The plan seems *practical practicable*.

16. That is the *latest last* letter.

17. That certainly was not a *human humane* action.

18. He *waited on waited for* his mother.

19. The *completeness completion* of the work brought many congratulations.

EXERCISE 82

Supply a word which will remedy the italicized impropriety in each of the following sentences. When in doubt consult a dictionary:

1. The *majority* of the illustrations are good.

2. No one can accurately *predicate* what the weather will be.

3. Shall you *except* the invitation?

4. They *claim* that the assertion cannot be proved.

5. They finally *located* the criminal in Dravosburg.

6. I shall *leave* you go at noon.

7. The *balance* of the essay was uninteresting.

8. By questions they tried to *eliminate* the true story.

9. They *impugn* false motives to me.

10. He was greatly *effected* by the news.

11. Sabbath *observation* was then very strict.

12. They *expect* that she wrote the letter.

13. The *invention* of electricity has revolutionized all manufactures.

14. Who *learned* her to sing?

15. Edison *discovered* the phonograph.

16. One cannot comprehend the *enormity* of a billion of dollars.

17. Many *complements* were paid to her beauty.

18. His *consciousness* pricked him.

19. How could any one be guilty of such a cruel *action*.

20. The *advancement* of the army was very slow.

195. Idioms. There are in English, as in other languages, a number of expressions that cannot be justified by the rules of grammar or rhetoric; and yet these expressions are among the most forcible ones in the language, and are continually used by the best writers. These expressions that lie outside all rules we call idioms. Compare the following idiomatic expressions with the unidiomatic expressions that succeed them. The second expression in each group is in accord with the strict rules of composition; but the first, the idiomatic, is far more forceful.

Idiomatic: The book which I read about.

Unidiomatic: The book about which I read.

Idiomatic: More than one life was lost.

Unidiomatic: More lives than one life were lost.

Idiomatic: Speak loud. Speak louder.

Unidiomatic: Speak loudly. Speak more loudly.

Idiomatic: A ten-foot pole.

Unidiomatic: A ten-feet pole.

Idiomatic: He strove with might and main.

Unidiomatic: He strove with might. (Might and main are two words of the same meaning.)

Idiomatic: He lectured on every other day.

Unidiomatic: He lectured on one day out of every two.

Idioms are not to be avoided. On the contrary, because they contribute great ease and force to composition, their use is to be encouraged. But the distinction between idiomatic and unidiomatic expressions is a fine one, and rests solely on usage. Care must be taken not to go beyond the idiomatic. There is probably little danger that the ordinary writer or speaker will not use idioms enough.

The following expressions are examples of commonly used idioms:

He was standing at the door *in his shirt sleeves*.

I *don't think* it will rain (I think it will not rain).

She walked out of the room *on her father's arm*.

John was a poor *shot*.

Do you feel *like a little candy*?

See what my foolishness has brought me *to*.

What part of the city will they settle *in*?

What was the house built *for*?

John needs a match to light his pipe *with*.

That is all I ask *for*.

What are you driving *at*?

Hard put to it.

By all odds.

Must needs.

I must *get up* by noon.

Get rid of.

Get used to.

Never so good.

Whether or no.

I can't go *either.*

You forget yourself when you speak so harshly.

I can come only *every other* day.

If the bell rings *answer the door.*

I take it that you will be there too.

Come and see me.

Try and do it.

The thief *took to his heels.*

196. Choice of Words. The words in which a thought is expressed may not offend against good use, and yet still be objectionable because they do not accurately and appropriately express the thought. One should choose not merely a word that will approximately express the thought, but the one word that best expresses it. The following suggestions are given to aid in the choice of words:

1. **Choose simple English words** and avoid what is called "fine writing." Young writers and newspaper writers are greatly given to this offense of fine or bombastic writing. Examples:

FINE WRITING	SIMPLE STYLE
Was launched into eternity	Was hanged
Disastrous conflagration	Great fire
Called into requisition the services of the family physician	Sent for the doctor
Was accorded an ovation	Was applauded
Palatial mansion	Comfortable house
Acute auricular perceptions	Sharp ears
A disciple of Izaak Walton	A fisherman

2. **Distinguish between general and specific terms.** In some cases general words may be used to advantage, but more often specific words should be used, since they call to the mind a definite image. Compare these sentences:

The *high color* of his face showed his embarrassment.

His *crimson* face showed his embarrassment.

He was a *large* man.

He was a *fat* man.

He was a man of *large frame*.

He was a *tall, heavily proportioned* man.

He was a man *six feet four inches tall* and *heavy* in proportion.

It was an *impressive* building.

It was a building of *impressive size*.

It was a building of *impressive beauty*.

His *fault* was robbery.

His *crime* was robbery.

3. **Avoid over-statement of facts.** The use of words that are too strong is a fault especially characteristic of Americans. Examples:

Poor: The concert was *simply exquisite*.

Better: The concert was *very good*.

Poor: She was *wild* over the mistake.

Better: She was *much annoyed* by the mistake.

4. **Avoid hackneyed phrases;** expressions that have been worked to death. Examples:

His paternal acres.

The infuriated beast.

The gentle zephyrs of springtime.

Was gathered to his fathers.

The blushing bride was led to the hymeneal altar.

Applauded to the echo.

EXERCISE 83

For each of the following expressions devise the best simple English expression that you can:

1. Individual was precipitated.
2. Tendered him a banquet.
3. At the witching hour of midnight.
4. The devouring element was checked.
5. Piscatorial sport.
6. Pedal extremities.
7. Fraught with tremendous possibilities.
8. Amid the plaudits of the multitude.
9. Caudal extremity.
10. Passed to his long home.
11. Dissected the Thanksgiving bird.
12. Presided at the organ.
13. Finger of scorn pointed at him.
14. Wended his way.
15. The green eyed monster.
16. The whole aggregation of knowledge chasers.
17. Maternal ancestor.
18. Shuffled off this mortal coil.
19. Failed to materialize at the banquet.
20. Tonsorial artist.
21. Twirler of the sphere.
22. Pugilistic encounters.
23. Performed his matutinal ablutions.

24. Partook of a magnificent collation.

25. Solemnized the rites of matrimony.

EXERCISE 84

In the third paragraph of the selection from Cranford (see §186) observe the use of the following words: **human, weakness, banks, twisted, annoyed,** *and* **undoing.** *Study the specific nature of these words by grouping about each of them other words of somewhat similar meaning, and then comparing the force of the various words in each group.*

This sort of exercise may be continued by choosing passages from any careful writer and studying the words that he has used.

EXERCISE 85

Substitute for each of the following expressions some expression that will be less general or less exaggerated:

1. She is *nice* looking.
2. We had a *perfectly gorgeous* time.
3. John is a *professional* man.
4. The play was *simply exquisite*.
5. To hear his voice makes me feel *funny*.
6. The opposing team was *completely annihilated*.
7. A *noise* caught our attention.
8. His manners are *horrid*.
9. We had a *great* time.
10. Such arrogance is *unendurable*.
11. That is a *good* book.

197. How to Improve One's Vocabulary. The few following suggestions may be found helpful in the acquiring of a good vocabulary:

1. Cultivate the dictionary habit. Learn the meaning, pronunciation, and spelling of each new word that you meet. Only when these three things are grasped about each word, does one really know the word. Some persons have found it an invaluable aid to carry with them a small note book or card on which they note down to be looked up at a convenient time words concerning which they are in doubt.

2. **In your writing and speaking use as much as possible the new words that you acquire.**

3. **Construct good English expressions** for all the slang, fine writing, and hackneyed phrases that you meet, and then use the good expressions instead of the bad ones.

4. **Study synonyms**; words of similar form and meaning. Only by a knowledge of synonyms can you express fine shades of meaning. *Crabbe's* English Synonyms and *Fernald's* Synonyms and Antonyms are good books of reference for this purpose. In addition to these books, lists of synonyms will be found in many books that are designed for general reference.

5. **Try to get the one word** that will best express the idea.

6. **Read good books** and good magazines, and read them carefully.

7. **Cultivate the society** of those who use good language.

EXERCISE 86

Look up the meaning of each of the words in the following groups of synonyms. Construct sentences in which each word is used correctly:

1. Love, like.
2. Wit, humor.
3. Discover, invent.
4. Observe, watch.
5. Pride, vanity, conceit.
6. Proof, evidence, testimony.
7. Balance, rest, remainder.
8. Word, term, expression.
9. Bring, fetch, carry.
10. Abandon, desert, forsake.
11. Propose, purpose, intend.
12. Healthful, healthy, wholesome.
13. Student, pupil, scholar.
14. Capacity, power, ability.
15. Blame, censure, criticism.
16. Accede, agree, yield, acquiesce.

17. Trickery, cunning, chicane, fraud.
18. Instruction, education, training, tuition.
19. Hardship, obstacle, hindrance, difficulty.
20. Maxim, precept, rule, law
21. Multitude, crowd, throng, swarm.
22. Delight, happiness, pleasure, joy.
23. Work, labor, toil, drudgery, task.
24. Silent, mute, dumb, speechless.
25. Kill, murder, assassinate, slay.
26. Hatred, enmity, dislike, ill-will.
27. Example, pattern, sample, model.
28. Obvious, plain, clear, apparent.
29. Noted, eminent, famous, prominent, notorious.
30. Old, aged, antique, ancient, antiquated, obsolete.

SPELLING

198. The following is a list of words that are frequently misspelled or confused. Where possible, an effort has been made to arrange them in groups in order that they may be more easily remembered. The word with an added ending has been used in most cases in place of the bare word itself as, *occasional* instead of *occasion*. A few rules have been included.

accede	descend	pressure
accident	fascinate	misspelled
accommodate	mischievous	possession
accordance	miscellaneous	
accuracy	muscle	recollection
succeed	susceptible	dispelled
occasional		miscellaneous
occur	existence	monosyllable
	experience	intellectual

across	sentence	parallel
amount		embellishment
apart	foregoing	wholly
arouse	forehead	woolly
		village
already	forty	villain
all right	foreign	till
	forfeit	
amateur	formally	perpetual
grandeur	formerly	persuade
		perspiration
appal	fulfill	
apparatus	willful	police
appetite		policies
approximate	guardian	
opportunity	guessing	presence
opposite		precede
disappoint	imminent	preceptor
disappearance	immediately	
	accommodation	fiend
choose	commission	siege
chosen	grammar	friend
	inflammation	yielding
boundary	recommend	
elementary	summary	seize

	symmetrical	receive
final	committee	receipt
finally		
usual	ledger	succeed
usually	legible	proceed
ascend	assassin	recede
ascent	dissimilar	secede
discerning	essential	accede
discipline	messenger	intercede
discontent		concede
discreet	necessary	supersede
descent	necessity	
	passport	

199. Words ending in a single consonant preceded by a single vowel, if monosyllables, or if the last syllable is accented, double the final consonant before the ending -*ed* and -*ing*, but not before -*ence*; as,

rob, rob*bed*, rob*bing*, rob*bers*.

confer, confer*red*, confer*ring*, confer*ence*.

transmit, transmit*ted*, transmit*ting*, transmi*ssion*.

impel, impel*led*, impel*ling*, imp*ulsion*.

Similar to the above are.

defer, infer, prefer, refer, transfer, occur (occurrence), abhor (abhorrence), omit, remit, permit, commit, beset, impel, compel, repel, excel (excellence), mob, sob, rub, skid.

If these words are not accented on the last syllable, the consonant is not doubled; as,

benefit, benefit*ed*, benefit*ing*, benefi*cial*.

Similar are:

differ, summon, model.

200. Words ending in silent *e* drop the *e* before a suffix beginning with a vowel; as,

arrive, arriv*ing*, arriv*ed*, arriv*al*.

precede, preced*ed*, preced*ing*, preced*ence*.

receive, receiv*ed*, receiv*ing*.

Similar are:

move, write, blame, tame, come, receive, believe, relieve, grieve, deceive, conceive, perceive, seize, precede, concede, supersede, recede, argue, rue, construe, woe, pursue.

201. Words ending in *-ge*, *-ce*, or *-se*, retain the *e* before endings: as,

arrange, arrangement; arrange, arranging.

Similar are:

gauge, manage, balance, finance, peace, service, amuse, use.

202. Words in *-dge* do not retain the *e* before endings; as, acknowledge, acknowledg*ment*, acknowledg*ed*, acknowledg*ing*.

Similar are:

nudge, judge.

203. Most words ending in *y* preceded by a consonant change *y* to *i* before all endings except-*ing*:

busy, bus*iness*, bus*ied*, busy*ing*.

Similar are:

duty, mercy, penny, pity, vary, weary, study.

204. Words of similar sound:

canvas (cloth)	principle (rule)
canvass (all meanings except *cloth*)	principal (chief)
capitol (a building)	stationary (immovable)
capital (all meanings except *building*)	stationery (articles)

counsel (advice or an adviser)
council (a body of persons)

complement (a completing element)
compliment (praise)

miner (a workman)
minor (under age)

angel (a spiritual being)
angle (geometrical)

205. Miscellaneous words:

annual	laundry	schedule
awkward	leisure	separate
beneficial	lenient	Spaniard
decimal	license	speak
exhilarate	mechanical	specimen
familiarize	mediæval	speech
fiber	medicine	spherical
fibrous	militia	subtle
genuine	motor	surely
gluey	negotiate	technical
height	origin	tenement
hideous	pacified	their
hundredths	phalanx	therefore
hysterical	physique	thinnest
icicle	privilege	until
irremediable	prodigies	vengeance
laboratory	rarefy	visible
laid	rinse	wherein
larynx	saucer	yielding

PRONUNCIATION

206. The following list is made up of words that are frequently mispronounced. An effort has been made to arrange them in groups according to the most frequent source of error in their pronunciation.

The only marks regularly used are the signs for the long and short sounds of the vowel.

ā as in *hate*   ī as in *high*   ū as in *use*

ă as in *hat*   ĭ as in *hit*   ŭ as in *run*

ē as in *me*   ō as in *old*   ōō as in *boot*

ĕ as in *met*   ŏ as in *hop*   ŏŏ as in *foot*

When sounds are not otherwise indicated take the sound that comes most naturally to the tongue.

207. ā as in *hate*:

Word	Correct Pronunciation
alma mater	*alma māter*
apparatus	*apparātus*
apricot	*āpricot*
attaché	*ăttashā'*
audacious	*audāshus*
ballet	*băl'lā*
blasé	*blazā'*
blatant	*blātant*
chasten	*chāsen*
Cleopatra	*Cleopātra*
compatriot	*compātriot*
gratis	*grātis* or *grahtis*

harem	*hārem* or *hahrem*
heinous	*hānous*
hiatus	*hiātus*
implacable	*implākable*
nape	*nāp*
née	*nā*
négligé	*nāglēzhā'*
patron	*pātron*
protégé	*prōtāzhā'*
résumé	*rāzumā'*
tenacious	*tenāshus*
tomato	*tomāto* or *tomahto*
valet	*vă'lā* or *văl'et*
vase	*vās, vahz,* or *vāz*
veracious	*verāshus*
vivacious	*vivāshus*

208. ă as in *hat*:

alternative	*ălternative*
Arab	*Ăr'ab*, not *ārab*
arid	*ăr'id*
asphalt	*asfălt*, not *fawlt*
bade	*băd*
catch	not *ketch*
defalcate	*defăl'kāte*, not *fawl*
dilletante	*dilletăn'te*

forbade	*forbăd*
granary	*grănary*
program	*pro'grăm*, not *grum*
rapine	*răp'ĭn*
rational	*rătional*
sacrament	*săcrament*

209. ä as in *arm*:

aunt	*änt*
behalf	*behäf*
calf	*käf*
calm	*käm*
half	*häf*
laugh	*läf*
psalm	*säm*

210. ē as in *me*:

amenable	*amēnable*
clique	*klēk*, not *klick*
creek	*krēk*, not *krick*
either	*ēēther* (preferable)
mediocre	*mēdiocre*
naïve	*na'ēve* (*a* as in *arm*)
neither	*nēēther* (preferable)
precedence	*precē'dence*
precedent	*prēcē'dent* (when an adjective)
predecessor	*prēdecessor*

predilection	*prēdilection*
premature	*prēmature*
quay	*kē*
resplendent	*rēsplen'dent*
sacrilegious	*sacrilēgious*, not *-religious*
series	*sērēz*
sleek	*slēk*, not *slick*
suite	*swēt*, not like *boot*

211. ĕ as in *met*:

again	*agĕn*
against	*agĕnst*
crematory	*krĕm'atōrȳ*
deaf	*dĕf*, not *dēf*
heroine	*hĕroĭn*, not like *hero*
measure	*mĕzhure*, not *mā*
metric	*mĕtrik*
precedent	*prĕc'edent* (noun)
prelate	*prĕl'āt*
presentation	*prĕzentation*
sesame	*sĕs'amē*
steady	*stĕdy*, not *stĭddy*
tenet	*tĕn'ĕt*
weapon	*wĕpon*, not *wēpon*

212. ī as in *high*:

appendicitis	*appendicītis*

biennial	*bīennial*
biography	*bīography*
bronchitis	*bronkītis*
carbine	*carbīne*
decisive	*decīsive*
demise	*demīse*
dynasty	*dī'năstў*
finis	*fīnis*
grimy	*grīmy*
hiatus	*hīā'tus*
inquiry	*inquī'ry*
long-lived	*long-līvd*
peritonitis	*peritonītis*
privacy	*prīvacy*
short-lived	*short-līvd*
simultaneous	*sīmultaneous*
tiny	*tīny*, not *tēny*

213. ĭ as in *hit*:

bicycle	*bī'sĭcle*
breeches	*brĭches*
breeching	*brĭching*
feminine	*femĭnĭn*
genuine	*genuĭn*
hypocrisy	*hĭpŏk'rĭsў*
italic	*ĭtăl'ĭk*

Italian	ĭtalyan
maritime	marĭtĭm
pretty	prĭtty
puerile	pū'erĭl
respite	rĕs'pĭt
tribune	trĭb'ŭn

214. ō as in *old*:

Adonis	Adōnis
apropos	aprōpō
bowsprit	bōwsprit
brooch	brōch not brōōsh
compromise	comprōmize
jowl	jōl, not like *owl*
molecular	mōlecular
ogle	ōgle
trow	trō
vocable	vōcable
zoology	zōology, not zōō

215. ŏ as in *hop*:

choler	kŏler
dolorous	dŏlorous
florid	flŏrid
molecule	mŏlecule
obelisk	ŏbelisk
probity	prŏbity

solecism	*sŏlesism*
solstice	*sŏlstice*
stolid	*stŏlid*

216. ōō as in *boot*:

bouquet	*bōōkā'*
canteloupe	*can'talōōp*
coup d'état	*kōō data'*
coupon	*kōō'pŏn*
ghoul	*gōōl*
hoof	*hōōf*
roof	*rōōf*
root	*rōōt*
route	*rōōt*
routine	*rōōtine*
wound	*wōōnd*

217. ū as in *use*:

accurate	*ăk'kūrāt*
culinary	*kūlinary*
gubernatorial	*gūbernatorial*
jugular	*jūgular*

218. ŭ as in *us*:

constable	*kŭnstable*
courtesan	*kŭr'tezăn*
hover	*hŭver*
iron	*iŭrn*

monetary	*mŭnetary*
nothing	*nŭthing*
wont	*wŭnt* (different from *won't*)

219. Miscellaneous words.

adobe	*adō'bā*
algebra	not *brā*
alien	*ālyen*, not *alien*
ameliorate	*amēlyorate*
antarctic	*antarktik*
anti	not *antī*
archangel	*arkangel*
archbishop	*arch*, not *ark*
arch fiend	*arch*, not *ark*
architect	*arkitect*
awkward	*awkward*, not *ard*
Beethoven	*bātōven*
Bingen	*Bĭng'en*
blackguard	*blag'gard*
Bowdoin	*bōdn*
brougham	*brōōm*
business	*bizness*
caldron	*kawldron*
calk	*kawk*
Cayenne	*kīen'*
courtier	*kortyer*

cuckoo	*kŏŏkōō*
dilemma	*dīlĕm'ma*
directly	not *dīrectly*
dishevelled	*dishev'ld*
Don Juan	*Don Jŭan* or *hōōan*
drought	*drowt*
drouth	*drowth*
extempore	*extĕmpore* (four syllables)
familiarity	*familyarity*
gaol	*jāl*
genealogy	*-alogy*, not *-ology*
gemus	*genyus*
Gloucester	*gloster*
gooseberry	*gōōz*, not *gōōs*
Hawaiian	*Hawī'yan* (*a* as in *arm*)
Helena	*hĕl'ena* (except *St. Helē'na*)
inconvenience	*inconvenyence*
Israel	*izrael*, not *issrael*
jeans	*jānes*
joust	*jŭst* or *jōōst*
larynx	*lăr'inx'* or *lā'rinx*, not *larnix*
literature	*literatūre*, or *chōōr*
Messrs.	*mĕshyerz* or *mĕsyerz*
Mineralogy	*-alogy*, not *-ology*
nature	*natūre*, or *chōōr*

oleomargarine	*g* is hard, as in *get*
orchid	*orkid*
oust	*owst*, not *ōōst*
peculiar	*pecūlyar*
pecuniary	*pēkūn'yărĭ*
perspiration	not *prespiratian*
prestige	*prĕs'tĭj* or *prĕstēzh'*
pronunciation	*pronunzēāshun* or *pronunshēāshun*
saucy	not *săssy*
schedule	*skedyŭl*
semi	not *semī*
theater	*thē'āter* not *thēā'ter*
turgid	*turjid*
usage	*uzage*
usurp	*uzurp*
vermilion	*vermilyun*
wife's	not *wives*
Xerxes	*zerxes*

220. Words with a silent letter:

almond	*ahmŭnd*
chasten	*chāsen*
chestnut	*chesnut*
glisten	*glissen*
kiln	*kill*

often	*ofen*
ostler	*ŏsler*
poignant	*poin'ant*
psalter	*sawlter*
salmon	*samun*
schism	*sism*
soften	*sofen*
subtle	*sutle*
sword	*sord*
thyme	*time*
toward	*tord*

221. Works chiefly of foreign pronunciation:

WORD	CORRECT PRONUNCIATION
bivouac	*biv'wak*
chargé d'affaires	*shar zhā'daffār'*
connoisseur	*connissur*
dishabille	*dis'abil*
ennui	*onwē*, not *ongwē*
finale	*finah'le*
foyer	*fwayā'*
massage	*masahzh*
naïve	*nah'ēv*
papier maché	*papyā mahshā*
piquant	*pē'kant*

prima facie	*prīma fā'shiē*
pro tempore	*prō těm'porē*
régime	*rāzhēm'*

222. Words often pronounced with a wrong number of syllables:

aerial	*āēreal*, not *ārēal*
athlete	two sylables, not *ath e lete*
attacked	*attakt*, two syllables
casualty	*kazh'ualte*, not *ality*
conduit	*cŏndit* or *kŏndit*, not *dōōit*
different	three syllables, not *diffrunt*
elm	not *ellum*
helm	not *hel um*
history	three syllables, not *histry*
honorable	not *honrable*
hygienic	*hy gi en' ic*, four syllables
interest	not *intrust*
interesting	not *intrusting*
ivory	not *ivry*
omelet	not *omlet*
realm	not *rellum*
separable	not *seprable*
ticklish	two syllables, not *tickelish*
valuable	*valuable*, not *valuble*
vaudeville	*vŏdvĭl*
Zeus	*zūs*, not *zēus*

223. Words accented on the first syllable:

admirable	*ad'mirable*
alias	*ā'lias*
applicable	*ap'plicable*
bicycle	*bī'sĭkle*
chastisement	*chas'tisement*
construe	*con'strue*
despicable	*des'picable*
desultory	*des'ultory*
disputant	*dis'putant*
exigency	*ex'ijency*
explicable	*ex'plicable*
exquisite	*ex'quisite*
extant	*ex'tant*
formidable	*for'midable*
Genoa	*jen'ōa*
gondola	*gon'dōla*
harass	*har'ass*
hospitable	*hos'pitable*
impious	*im'pious*, not *impīous*
industry	*in'dustry*
inventory	*in'ventory*
lamentable	*lam'entable*
mischievous	*mis'chievous*
obligatory	*ob'ligatory*

pariah	*pa'riah*
peremptory	*per'emptory*
preferable	*pref'erable*
Romola	*Rōm'ola*
vehemence	*vē'hemence*

224. Words accented on the second syllable:

WORD	CORRECT PRONUNCIATION
abdomen	*abdō'men*
acclimate	*acclī'mate*
acumen	*acū'men*
albumen	*albū'men*
artificer	*artif'iser*
bitumen	*bitū'men*
chicanery	*shikā'nery*
illustrate	*illus'trate*
incognito	*ĭnkŏg'nĭtō*
incomparable	*incom'parable*
indisputable	*indis'putable*
inexorable	*inex'orable*
inexplicable	*inex'plicable*
inhospitable	*inhos'pitable*
inquiry	*inqui'ry*
irrevocable	*irrev'ocable*
misconstrue	*miscon'strue*

nitrogenous	*nītroj'enous*
opponent	*oppo'nent*
pianist	*pian'ist*
refutable	*refut'able*
syllabic	*syllab'ic*
telegraphy	*teleg'raphy*
vagary	*vagā'ry*
Yosemite	*yō sĕm' ĭ te*

225. Words accented on the last syllable:

address	*address'*
adept	*adept'*
adult	*adult'*
ally	*ally'*
commandant	*commandänt' (ä as in arm)*
contour	*contour'*
dessert	*dessert'*
dilate	*dilate'*
excise	*ĕksīz'*
finance	*finance'*
grimace	*grimāce'*
importune	*importūne'*
occult	*occult'*
pretence	*prētence'*
research	*rēsearch'*
robust	*rōbust'*

romance	*rō'mance'*
tirade	*tī'rade'*

226. Words whose pronunciation depends on meaning:

accent   *Accent'* the first syllable.

         Place the *ac'cent* upon the first syllable.

aged   An *a'ged* man.

         Properly *aged* wine (one syllable).

blessed   The *bless'ed* saints.

         Let them be *blessed* (one syllable).

contrast   The strange *con'trast*.

         Contrast' the two.

converse   Did you *converse'* with him?

         Is the *con'verse* true?

desert   The sandy *des'ert*.

         They *desert'* their friends.

learned   He *learned* (one syllable) to sing.

         A *learn ed* man.

precedent   A *prēcē'dent* place.

         It establishes a *prĕc'edent*.

project   A new *proj'ect*.

         To *project'* from.

GLOSSARY OF MISCELLANEOUS ERRORS

Admire. Do not use *admire* in the sense of *like*.

Wrong: I should *admire* to be able to do that.

Right: I should *like* to be able to do that.

Aggravate. Do not use *aggravate* in the sense of *irritate* or *disturb*. *Aggravate* means *to make worse*.

Wrong: His impudence *aggravates* me.

Right: His impudence *irritates* me.

Ain't. *Ain't* and *hain't* are never proper as contractions of *am not*, *is not*, or *are not*.

Allow. Do not use *allow* in the sense of *assert*, *say*, or *intend*.

Wrong: He *allowed* that he had better start. I *allow* to be back before noon.

Right: He *said* that he had better start. I *intend* to be back before noon.

Allude. Do not use *allude* in the sense of *refer*. To *allude* to a thing means to refer to it in an indirect way.

Wrong: He *alluded* by name to John Milton.

Right: He *alluded* to Milton by the term "Blind Poet."

Any. Do not use *any* in the sense of *at all* or *to any degree*.

Wrong: Because of the injury he can not see *any*.

As. Do not use *as* for the relative pronouns *who* and *that*.

Wrong: I am the man *as* digs your garden. Not *as* I remember.

Right: I am the man *who* digs your garden. Not *that* I remember.

As. Do not use *as* in the sense of *since* or *because*.

Wrong: I cannot come *as* I am sick now.

Right: I cannot come; I am sick now.

Right: I cannot come *because* I am sick now.

At. Do not use *at* for *in* with the names of large cities

Wrong: He lives *at* Philadelphia.

Right: He lives *in* Philadelphia.

Attackted. Do not use this form for *attacked*.

Awful, awfully. These are two very much overworked words. Substitute other and more accurate expressions.

Wrong: We have had an *awfully* good time. That is an *awfully* pretty dress.

Right: We have had an *exceedingly* nice time. That is a *very* pretty dress.

Badly. Do not use *badly* in the sense of *very much*.

Wrong: She wanted *badly* to come.

Right: She wanted *very much* to come.

Beside, besides. *Beside* means *next to*. *Besides* means *in addition to*.

Right: John lives *beside* his mother.

Right: *Besides* the daughters, there are three sons.

Between. Do not use *between* when referring to more than two objects.

Wrong: There is bad feeling *between* the members of the class.

Right: There is bad feeling *among* the members of the class.

Blowed. Do not use *blowed* for *blew* or *blown*. There is no such word.

Best. Do not use *best* when only two objects are referred to. Use *better*. *Best* should be used only when more than two are referred to.

Wrong: He is the *best* of the two brothers.

Right: He is the *better* of the two brothers.

Right: He is the *best* of the three brothers.

Bound. Do not use *bound* for *determined*.

Wrong: He was *bound* to go skating.

Right: He was *determined* to go skating.

Right: He *bound* himself to pay three hundred dollars.

But. Do not use *but* after a negative in the sense of *only*. See §**46**.

Wrong: There *isn't but* one apple left.

Right: There *is but* one apple left.

Calculate. Do not use *calculate* in the sense of *think*, *expect*, or *intend*.

Can. Do not use *can* to denote permission. It denotes ability or possibility. *May* denotes permission. See §**69**

Wrong: *Can* I speak to you for a minute?

Right: *May* I speak to you for a moment?

Character, reputation. Do not confuse these two words. *Character* means one's moral condition. *Reputation* means the morality that others believe one to possess.

Clum. There is no such form of the verb *climb*.

Complected. Do not use *complected* for *complexioned*. See §**40**.

Conclude. Do not use conclude in the sense of *forming an intention*.

Right: Finally, I *decided* to go home.

Right: I was forced to *conclude* that I had made an error.

Considerable. Do not use *considerable* in the sense of *very much*.

Wrong: This lesson is *considerable* better than yesterday's.

Cute. A much overworked word. Use some expression that is more accurate; as, *pretty*, *amusing*, etc.

Decease, disease. Do not confuse *decease* and *disease*. The first means *death*, the second *sickness*. *The deceased* means a person who is dead.

Wrong: The *diseased* will be buried at four o'clock.

Wrong: The property of the *diseased* will be sold at auction.

Decease. Do not use *decease* as a verb in the sense of *die*.

Wrong: His father *deceased* last year.

Demand. *Demand* should not have a person as its object.

Wrong: He *demanded* John to pay.

Right: He *demanded* payment from John. He *demanded* that John pay.

Different. Use the preposition *from* after *different*, not *than*.

Don't. Do not use *don't* with a subject in the third person singular. See §64.

Down. Do not use *down* as a verb in the sense of *defeat* or *overthrow*.

Wrong: Our football team *has downed* every other team in the state.

Right: Our football team *has defeated* every other team in the state.

Drownded. *Drownded* is not a proper form of the verb *drown*. Say *drowned*. (Pronounced *drownd*.)

Each other. Do not use *each other* to refer to more than two objects. See §44.

Wrong: The members of the regiment helped *each other*.

Right: The members of the regiment helped *one another*.

Effect, affect. Do not confuse *effect* and *affect*. *Effect* means *a result*, or *to cause a thing to be done*. *Affect* means *to disturb* or *have an influence on*.

Wrong: The news *effected* him seriously.

Right: The news *affected* him seriously.

Wrong: The *affect* of this news was to cause war.

Right: The *effect* of this news was to cause war.

Either. Do not use *either* with reference to more than two objects, nor follow it by a plural verb. See §43.

Wrong: *Either* of the three will do. *Either* you or John *have* done it.

Right: *Any one* of the three will do. *Either* you or John *has* done it.

Emigrate, immigrate. Do not confuse *emigrate* and *immigrate*. To *emigrate* means *to go out of a place*, to *immigrate* means *to come into a place*.

Right: The Italians *emigrate* from their country.

Right: Of those who *immigrate* to America, a large number are Italians.

Enough. Do not follow *enough* by a clause beginning with *that* or *so that*.

Wrong: I studied *enough* that I could recite the lesson.

Right: I studied *enough to* recite the lesson.

Enthuse. Do not use *enthuse* in the sense of to create enthusiasm.

Wrong: He tried to *enthuse* his audience.

Right: He tried to *arouse* enthusiasm in his audience.

Etc. *Etc.* stands for *et cetera*, and means *and so forth*. Do not spell it *ect*. Do not use it in composition that is intended to be elegant.

Everybody. *Everybody* should not be followed by a plural verb or a plural pronoun. See §21.

Except, accept. Do not confuse these two words. *Accept* means *to acknowledge*. *Except* means *to exclude*.

Right: I cannot *accept* such slovenly work.

Wrong: I *except* your apology.

Except. Do not use *except* for *unless*. See §85.

Wrong: I can not sleep *except* it is quiet.

Expect. Do not use *expect* in the sense of *suppose* or *think*.

Wrong: I *expect* you have read that book.

Right: I *suppose* you have read that book.

Fine. Do not use *fine* in place of some more definite word. *Fine* is a much over-worked word.

Wrong: The book is *fine* for class-room work.

Right: The book is *well adapted* for class-room work.

Firstly. *Firstly* should never be used. Say *first*. See §40.

First-rate. Do not use *first-rate* as an adverb in the sense of *very well*.

Wrong: That does *first-rate*.

Right: That does *very well*.

Right: He is a *first-rate fellow*.

Former. Do not use *former* when more than two are referred to. Say *first*. See §41.

From. Do not use *from* with *whence, hence* and *thence*.

Wrong: *From whence* have you come?

Right: *Whence* have you come? *From where* have you come?

Funny. Do not use *funny* for *singular* or *strange*. *Funny* is an overworked word.

Wrong: It is *funny* that he died.

Right: It is *singular* that he died.

Gent. Do not use the word at all. Say *gentleman* or *man*.

Gentleman. Do not use *gentleman* to denote sex only. Say *man*. *Gentleman* is properly used, however, to denote a person of refinement.

Wrong: Only *gentlemen* are allowed to vote in Pennsylvania.

Right: Mr. Lincoln was a *gentleman* in the true sense of the word.

Got. Do not use got with *have* or *had* to indicate merely *possession* or *obligation*. *Got* means acquired through effort.

Wrong: I *have got* the measles. You *have got* to do it.

Right: I *have* the measles. You *must* do it.

Right: After much study I *have got* my lesson.

Grand. Do not use *grand* in place of some more definite and accurate expression. It is another over-worked word.

Wrong: We have had a *grand time* this afternoon.

Right: We have had a *very pleasant* time this afternoon.

Guess. Do not use *guess* in the sense of *think* or *suppose*.

Wrong: I *guess* the trains are late to-day.

Right: I *suppose* the trains are late to-day.

Right: Can you *guess* the riddle?

Had ought. Do not use *had* with *ought*. See §54.

Hardly. Do not use *hardly* after a negative. See §46.

Wrong: I *can not hardly* believe that.

Right: I *can hardly* believe that.

Have. Do not use *have* after *had*.

Wrong: If I *had have been* able to go.

Right: If I *had been* able to go.

Heighth. Do not use *heighth* for *height*.

Hung. Do not confuse *hung* and *hanged*. *Hanged* is the proper word to use in reference to executions.

Wrong: He was condemned *to be hung*.

Right: He was condemned *to be hanged*.

Right: The picture was *hung* in the parlor.

Humbug. Do not use *humbug* as a verb.

Wrong: He has *humbugged* the people for years.

Illy. Do not use *illy* for the adverb *ill*. See §40.

In, into. Do not confuse *in* and *into*.

Wrong: He went *in* the house.

Right: He went *into* the house.

Right: He exercised *in* a gymnasium.

Kind. Do not precede kind by *those* or *these*.

Wrong: I do not like *those kind* of plays.

Right: I do not like *that kind* of play.

Kind of a. Do not use *a* or *an* after *kind of*. See §47.

Wrong: It is *one kind of* a mistake.

Right: It is *one kind of* mistake.

Lady. Do not use *lady* to designate sex only. It is properly used to indicate persons of refinement.

Wrong: Is Mrs. Johnson a colored *lady*?

Right: Is Mrs. Johnson a colored *woman*?

Right: Mrs. Johnson is a colored *woman*, and *a lady*.

Latter. Do not use *latter* to refer to more than two objects. Use *last*. See §41.

Lay. Do not confuse *lay* and *lie*. See §57.

Learn. Do not confuse *learn* and *teach*. *Learn* means *to acquire knowledge*. *Teach* means *to impart knowledge*.

Wrong: He can *learn* you as much as any one can.

Right: He can *teach* you as much as any one can.

Leave. Do not confuse *leave* and *let*. Leave means *to let remain*. Let means *to give permission*.

Wrong: Will your mother *leave* you go?

Right: Will your mother *let* you go?

Right: I shall *leave* my trunk in my room.

Liable. Do not use *liable* for *likely*.

Wrong: It is *liable* to rain to-day.

Right: It is *likely* to rain to-day.

Right: He is *liable* for all that he has agreed to pay.

Lightning. Do not use *lightning* as a verb in place of *lightens*.

Wrong: During the storm, it *lightnings* frequently.

Right: During the storm, it *lightens* frequently.

Like. Do not use *like* for *as*. *Like* is a preposition. *As* is a conjunction.

Wrong: He doesn't talk *like* he did yesterday.

Right: He doesn't talk *as* he did yesterday.

Right: It looks *like* a mahogany chair.

Lit on. Do not use *lit on* in the sense of *met with* or *discovered*.

Wrong: I at last *lit on* this plan.

Lot. Do not use *lot* in the sense of *a great number* or *a great deal*.

Wrong: A *lot* of people were there, She talks *a lot*.

Most. Do not use *most* for *almost*.

Wrong: I have *most* completed the book.

Right: I have *almost* completed the book.

Right: He has done *the most* of the work.

Mrs. Do not use *Mrs.* before titles; as, Mrs. President, Mrs. Professor, Mrs. Doctor.

Much. Do not use *much* for *many*. *Much* refers to quantity. *Many* refers to number.

Wrong: As *much as* five hundred people were present.

Right: As *many as* five hundred people were present.

Mutual. Do not confuse *mutual* and *common*. *Mutual* means *interchanged*.

Wrong: John and William had a *mutual* liking for Mary.

Right: John and William had a *common* liking for Mary.

Right: John and William had a *mutual* liking for each other.

Near. Do not use *near* for *nearly*.

Wrong: He ran *near* all the way to the station. I came *nearly* making the same mistake.

Right: He ran *nearly* all the way to the station. I came *near* making the same mistake.

Nerve. Do not use *nerve* in the sense of *impudence*.

Newsy. Do not use *newsy* in the sense of *full of news*.

Neither. Do not use *neither* with reference to more than two objects, nor follow it by a plural verb.

Wrong: *Neither* of the three could come. *Neither* of the two *are* here.

Right: *No one* of the three could come. *Neither* of the two *is* here.

No good. Do not use *no good* in the sense of *worthless* or *not good.*

Wrong: The book is *no good.*

No place. Do not use *no place* after a negative. See §46.

Wrong: I am not going *no place.*

Right: I am not going *anywhere.* I *am going nowhere.*

Notorious. Do not use *notorious* in the sense of *famous* or *noted. Notorious* means of *evil reputation.*

Wrong: Gladstone was a *notorious* statesman of England.

Right: Several *notorious thieves* were arrested.

Nowhere near. Do not use *nowhere near* for *not nearly.* See §40.

Wrong: *Nowhere near* so many people came as were expected.

Right: *Not nearly* so many people came as were expected.

Right: James was *nowhere near* the scene of the fire.

Of. Do not use *of* for *have* in such expressions as *could, have, might have, should have,* etc.

Wrong: If I *could of* been there.

Right: If I *could have* been there.

Only. Guard against the improper use of *only* after a negative. See §46.

Wrong: There *are not only* four books on that subject.

Right: There *are only* four books on that subject.

Outside of. Do not use *outside of* for *aside from.*

Wrong: *Outside of* James, all had a good time.

Right: *Aside from* James, all had a good time.

Over with. Do not use *over with* for *over.*

Wrong: I must write the letter and have it *over with.*

Pants. Do not use the word *pants* for *trousers.*

Photo. Do not use *photo* for *photograph.*

Piece. Do not use *piece* in the sense of *way* or *distance*.

Wrong: I shall walk a *little piece* with you.

Right: I shall walk a *little way* with you.

Place. Do not use *place* after *any, every, no*, etc., in the sense of *anywhere, everywhere, nowhere*, etc.

Wrong: I can not find it *any place*.

Right: I can not find it *anywhere*.

Plenty. Do not use *plenty* as an adjective or an adverb.

Wrong: Money is *plenty*. He is *plenty able* to do it.

Right: Money is *plentiful*. He is *quite able* to do it.

Poorly. Do not use *poorly* for *ill* or *bad*.

Wrong: He feels very *poorly*.

Principle, principal. Do not confuse *principle* and *principal*. *Principle* means a *rule* or *truth*. *Principal* means *leader, chief, the most important*.

Propose. Do not use *propose* in the sense of *intend*.

Wrong: I *propose* to tell all I know.

Right: I *intend* to tell all I know.

Providing. Do not use *providing* for *if* or *on the condition*.

Wrong: I will go *providing* you can get tickets for three.

Right: I will go *on the condition that* you get the tickets.

Raise, rise. Do not confuse *raise* with *rise*. See §57.

Recommend, recommendation. Do not use *recommend* as a noun. *Recommendation* is the noun.

Wrong: Her employer gave her a good *recommend*.

Right: Her employer gave her a good *recommendation*.

Right away, right off. Do not use *right away* or *right off* in the sense of *immediately*.

Wrong: After the play we will come *right off*.

Right: After the play we will come *at once*.

Same. Do not use *same* as a pronoun.

Wrong: I will write the letter and mail *same* at once.

Right: I will write the letter and mail *it* at once.

Say. Do not use *say* in the sense of *order* or *command*.

Wrong: Your mother *said for* you to come home at once.

Right: Your mother *said that* you should come home at once.

Scarcely. Do not use *scarcely* after a negative. See §46.

Wrong: There *was not scarcely* a pound of meat for us all.

Right: There *was scarcely* a pound of meat for us all.

Seldom ever. Do not use *seldom* with *ever*. Say instead *seldom* or *seldom, if ever*.

Wrong: Fires *seldom ever* occur.

Right: Fires *seldom* occur. Fires *seldom, if ever* occur.

Shut of. Do not use *shut of* in the sense of *rid of*.

Wrong: We are *shut of* him at last.

Sight. Do not use *sight* in the sense of *many* or *much*.

Wrong: A great *sight of people* flocked to hear him.

Right: A great *many people* flocked to hear him.

Sit, set. Do not confuse these two words. See §57.

So. Do not use *so* alone as a conjunction. Say *so that*.

Wrong: He spoke in the open air, *so* more could see and hear him.

Right: He spoke in the open air, *so that* more could see and hear him.

Some. Do not use *some* as an adverb in the sense of *somewhat* or a *little*.

Wrong: He plays the violin *some*.

Right: He plays the violin *a little*.

Sort of a. Do not use *a* after *sort of*. See *Kind of a*.

Sort. Do not precede *sort* by *these* or *those*. See *Kind*.

Such. Do not follow *such* by *who*, *which*, or *that* as relatives.

Wrong: All *such persons who* think so will soon see their mistake.

Right: All *such persons as* think so will soon see their mistake.

Right: He spoke with *such* force *that* we were compelled to listen. (*That* is not a relative here.)

Tasty. Do not use *tasty* in the sense of *tasteful*.

That. Do not use *that* as an adverb.

Wrong: I did not think the book was *that* small.

Right: I did not think that the book was *so* small.

That there, this here, these here, those there. *There* and *here*, in all these expressions are worse than unnecessary.

Them there. Do not use *them there* for *those*.

Wrong: Bring me *them there* books.

Right: Bring me *those* books.

Three first, two first, etc. Do not say *three first*, but *first three*. There can be only one *first*.

Too. Do not use *too* alone before a verb or a participle.

Wrong: He is *too excited* to listen to you.

Right: He is *too much excited* to listen to you.

Very. Do not use *very* alone before a verb or a participle.

Wrong: You are *very* mistaken.

Right: You are *very much* mistaken.

Wait on, wait for. Do not confuse these two expressions. *Wait on* means *to serve*. *Wait for* means *to await*.

Wrong: Do not *wait on* me if I do not come at noon.

Right: Do not *wait for* me if I do not come at noon.

Wake, awake. Do not confuse *wake* and *awake*. See §57.

Milton Keynes UK
Ingram Content Group UK Ltd.
UKHW010631080624
443649UK00030B/549